前言

拉宾德拉纳特·泰戈尔是印度著名诗人、文学家、社会活动家、哲学家和印度民族主义者。1913年，他以诗集《吉檀迦利》成为第一位获得诺贝尔文学奖的亚洲人。他的代表作有《吉檀迦利》《飞鸟集》《眼中沙》《家庭与世界》《园丁集》《新月集》《最后的诗篇》《文明的危机》等。

泰戈尔是印度著名诗人也是具有巨大世界影响的作家。在他的一生中，他共创作了50多部诗集，被称为"诗圣"。泰戈尔在诗歌、体裁、语言及表现方法上大胆创新，独具一格。他还善于学习和运用人民生活中的口头语言，使诗歌的语言清新活泼。瑞典诗人魏尔纳·冯·海登斯塔姆这样评价泰戈尔的《吉檀迦利》："我不记得过去二十多年我是否读过如此优美的抒情诗歌，我从中真不知道得到多么久远的享受，仿佛我正在饮着一股清凉而新鲜的泉水。在它们的每一种思想和感情所显示的炽热和爱的纯洁中，心灵的清澈，风格的优美和自然的激情，所有这一切都水乳交融，揭示出了一种完整的、深刻的、罕见的精神美。"

西蒂翻译的《飞鸟集》是泰戈尔的第一部中文诗集。《飞鸟集》出版后，中国诗坛上开始流行一种表现随感的短诗，比如冰心创作的《繁星》《春水》等。

冰心在1955年翻译了泰戈尔的《吉檀迦利》，她称赞说："泰戈尔是诞生于歌鸟之巢的孩子，从他欢乐的心境中，他热爱着周围的一切。他用绚烂美丽的诗歌，来歌唱他所热爱的大自然和人类。"

这些晶莹清丽、带有哲理的小诗赢得了很多人的喜爱，几乎影响了一代诗风。诗人徐志摩在泰戈尔1924年访华期间，以翻译的身份全程陪同左右。两人一见之下即引为知己，成为二十世纪诗坛上著名的"忘年交"。他说："跟泰戈尔老人在一起，我的灵感就有了翅膀，总是立刻就能找到最好的感觉。"

泰戈尔的诗集使我们明白，美往往就在我们的隔壁，最不经意，也最简朴。挪动你的脚步，叩响那扇门，你会发现生活是如此的可爱。我们可以清晰地感受到他对光明的向往、对人生的思考、对生活的憧憬以及对大自然的热爱。他让我们相信，生活中不是缺少美，而是缺少发现美的眼睛。只要心中充满爱，我们就不会孤独与彷徨。

目录

第一卷 开始

飞鸟集 / 6
流萤集 / 16
园丁集 / 24
新月集 / 28
The Beginning / 开始 28
Vocation / 职业 32
Baby's Way / 孩童之道 34
The Judge / 审判官 38
吉檀迦利 / 40
Innocence / 无知 40
The Voice / 你的声音 42
The Wayside Where Shadow Chases Light / 影逐光的地方 44
Your Pour / 你的倾注 46
Drunk with the Joy of Singing / 在歌唱中陶醉 48
My Heart Longs to Join in Thy Song / 我的心渴望与你合唱 50

Come Out of Thy Meditations / 从静坐中走出来罢 52
Light, Oh Where Is the Light? / 灯火，灯火在哪里呢？ 54
Where Dost Thou Stand Behind Them All / 你站在大家背后 56
He Comes, Comes / 他正在走来，走来 60
Beautiful Is Thy Wristlet / 你的手镯真是美丽 62
A Kingly Jest / 一个天大的玩笑 64
It Is Time to Sit Quite / 静坐的时光 66
When I Try to Bow to Thee / 我想向你鞠躬 68
I Kept Her in My Heart / 我将她深藏于心 70
I Am Here to Sing Thee Songs / 我来为你唱歌 72
It Is Only For Thee That I Hope / 我只企望你 74

鲜花与尘土
——泰戈尔哲理诗选

【印】泰戈尔 著　冰心 等 译

江苏凤凰科学技术出版社·南京

图书在版编目（CIP）数据

鲜花与尘土：泰戈尔哲理诗选：汉英对照 /（印）泰戈尔著；冰心等译 . — 南京：江苏凤凰科学技术出版社，2015.11（2022.5 重印）
（易人外语）
ISBN 978-7-5537-5473-4

Ⅰ．①鲜… Ⅱ．①泰…②冰… Ⅲ．①英语 - 阅读教学 - 自学参考资料②诗集 - 印度 - 现代 Ⅳ．① H319.4：I

中国版本图书馆 CIP 数据核字 (2015) 第 230818 号

易人外语
鲜花与尘土——泰戈尔哲理诗选

著　　　者	【印】泰戈尔
译　　　者	冰　心　等
责 任 编 辑	祝　萍
责 任 监 制	方　晨

出 版 发 行	江苏凤凰科学技术出版社
出版社地址	南京市湖南路 1 号 A 楼，邮编：210009
出版社网址	http://www.pspress.cn
印　　　刷	天津丰富彩艺印刷有限公司
开　　　本	880 mm × 1 230 mm　1/32
印　　　张	10
字　　　数	150 000
版　　　次	2015 年 11 月第 1 版
印　　　次	2022 年 5 月第 2 次印刷
标 准 书 号	ISBN 978-7-5537-5473-4
定　　　价	45.00 元

图书如有印装质量问题，可随时向我社印务部调换。

第二卷　迷失的星星

飞鸟集 / 78
流萤集 / 88
采果集 / 94
园丁集 / 98
吉檀迦利 / 102
Lost Star / 迷失的星星 102
Thou Keepest Me Free / 你让我自由 104
Journey Home / 倦旅的家 106
I Live in the Hope of Meeting with Him / 我生活在与他相会的希望中 108
My Desires Are Many / 我的欲望很多 110
Deity of the Ruined Temple / 破庙里的神呵 112
I Love This Life / 我爱今生 114
I Will Deck Thee with Trophies / 我要以胜利品来装饰你 116

You and Me / 你和我 118
He It Is / 就是他 120
Time Is Endless in Thy Hands / 你手里的时光是无限的 122
Useless Lamp / 无用之灯 124
Thou Givest Thyself to Me in Love / 你把自己在梦中交给了我 126
O Thou Beautiful / 呵，美丽的你 128
The Arrival of the King / 国王的到来 130
Thy Dreadful Sword / 你的可畏的剑 132
Oh Awaken！/ 呵，醒来罢！136
I Stood Silent / 我静静地站立 138
Lies / 谎言 140
The Gorgeous Constraint / 华美的约束 142
Full of Sorrow / 离愁弥漫 144

第三卷　不再高声喧哗

飞鸟集 / 148
流萤集 / 158
园丁集 / 164
吉檀迦利 / 170
No More Noisy Lord Words / 不再高声喧哗 170
Closed Path / 山穷水尽 172
Lost Time / 蹉跎岁月 174
Let Me Not Forget a Moment / 让我念念不忘 176
In One Salutation to Thee / 在我向你合十膜拜 178
And You Sit There Smiling / 你却坐在那里微笑 180

I Sought Thee with My Songs / 我以诗歌来寻求你 182
Waiting For Him in Vain / 等他又落了空 184
My King / 我的国王 186
I Am Eager to Die into the Deathless / 我渴望死于不死之中 188
At This Time of My Parting / 在我动身的时光 190
Come Silently and Take Thy Seat Here / 悄悄地走来坐下罢 192
I Find Her Not / 我找不到她 194
Whisper to Me！/ 对我低语罢！196
I Must Launch Out My Boat / 我必须撑出我的船去 198

Do Not Pass by Like a Dream / 不要像梦一般地走过 200
We Sail in a Boat Together / 我们一同去泛舟 202
When One Knows Thee / 当有人认识了你 204
Is It Beyond Thee to Be Glad with This Rhythm？/ 这音律不能使你高兴吗？206
I Have No Sleep Tonight / 我今夜无眠 208

第四卷　面对面

飞鸟集 / 212
流萤集 / 222
园丁集 / 230
吉檀迦利 / 236
O Fool / 呵，傻子 236
Give Me Strength / 赐予我力量 238
Face to Face / 面对面 240
Beggarly Heart / 赤贫之心 242
Pluck This Little Flower / 采下这朵小花 244
I Am Only Waiting For Love / 我只等候着爱 246
Freedom Is All I Want / 我只要自由 248
Prisoner, Tell Me / 囚人，告诉我 250
Let My Country Awake / 让我的国家觉醒吧 252
That I Want Thee, Only Thee / 我需要你，只需要你 254
Call Back, My Lord / 请你召回，我的主 256
The Baby / 婴儿 258
I Do Not Know Thee As My Own / 我不知道你是属于我的 260
Where Had They Hid Their Power？/ 他们的武力藏在哪里呢？262
Death / 死亡 264
I Will Never Shut the Doors of My Senses / 我永不会关上我感觉的门户 266

第五卷　最后的帷幕

飞鸟集 / 270
流萤集 / 280
园丁集 / 286
吉檀迦利 / 294
Purity / 纯洁 294
The Last Curtain / 最后的帷幕 296
Thy Gifts to Us Mortals / 你赐给我们世人的礼物 298
Who Is He? / 他是谁？300
Stream of Life / 生命的溪流 302
You stood at my cottage door / 你站在我的草舍门前 304
Look Forward to You / 期待你 306
Farewell / 辞别 308
Gloaming / 黄昏 310
Let Only That Little Be Left of Me / 只要我一息尚存 312
Thou Lord of All Heavens / 你这万王之王 314
When Death Will Knock at Thy Door / 当死神来叩你门的时候 316

第一卷 开始

飞鸟集

1

Life finds its wealth by the claims[1] of the world,
and its worth by the claims of love.

热词天地

1. claim [kleɪm] **vt.** 声称；断言；需要；索取

生命从世界获取财富，
爱情使它富于价值。

2

Do not seat your love upon a precipice[1] because it is high.

热词天地

1.precipice ['presəpɪs] *n.* 悬崖，峭壁

不要因为峭壁很高，就将你的爱情置于其上。

3

O Beauty, find thyself in love, not in the flattery of thy mirror.

热词天地

flattery ['flætərɪ] *n.* 奉承（话）

啊，美呀，你要在爱中找寻自己，不要觅之于镜子的阿谀。

4

Chastity[1] is a wealth that comes from abundance of love.

热词天地

1. chastity ['tʃæstətɪ] *n.* 纯洁，贞洁

贞洁是来自富足的爱的财富。

5

Every child comes with the message that God is not yet discouraged[1] of man.

热词天地

1. discouraged [dɪs'kʌrɪdʒd] *adj.* 灰心的；沮丧的；气馁的

每个孩子出生时都带来信息说——
神对人并未灰心失望。

6

My heart beats her waves at the shore of the world and writes upon it her signature[1] in tears with the words, "I love thee."

热词天地

1.signature ['sɪgnətʃə(r)] *n.* 签名；署名

我的心把她的波浪在世界的海岸上冲激着，
以热泪在上面写下她的题记："我爱你。"

7

Power said to the world, "You are mine."
The world kept it prisoner on her throne[1].
Love said to the world, "I am thine[2]."
The world gave it the freedom of her house.

热词天地

1. throne [θrəʊn] *n.* 宝座；御座；王位；王权
2. thine [ðaɪn] *pron.* 你的东西，你的

权力对世界说："你是我的。"
世界便把权力囚禁在她的宝座下面。
爱情对世界说："我是你的。"
世界便给了爱情在她屋内的自由。

8

Love! when you come with the burning lamp[1] of pain in your hand,

I can see your face and know you as bliss[2].

热词天地

1.lamp [læmp] *n.* 灯；发热灯，照射灯
2.bliss [blɪs] *n.* 极乐；天赐的福

爱情啊，当你举着燃烧的苦痛之灯走来时，
我能够看见你的脸，
而且深知你是赐福。

9

Once we dreamt that we were strangers.

We wake up to find that we were dear to each other.

梦中我们互不相识。
醒来我们亲密无间。

10

The world does not leak[1] because death is not a crack[2].

热词天地
1.leak [liːk] *vi.* 漏出；透露
2.crack [kræk] *vt.* 破裂，打开

世界不会流失，因为死亡并不是一个罅隙。

11

"I cannot keep your waves, "says the bank to the river,
"Let me keep your footprints in my heart."

"我留不住你的海浪，"岸堤对河流说，
"让我把你的脚印留在我的心里吧！"

12

I am a child in the dark.
I stretch my hands through the coverlet[1] of night for thee, Mother.

热词天地

1.coverlet ['kʌvələt] *n.* 床罩

我是一个身处黑暗中的孩子。
我穿过夜的被单向您伸出我的双手,母亲。

13

Let the dead have the immortality[1] of fame,
but the living the immortality of love.

热词天地

1.immortality [ˌɪmɔːˈtæləti] *n.* 不朽；不朽的声名

让亡者有那不朽的名，
让生者有那不朽的爱。

14

Love is life in its fullness like the cup
with its wine.

爱就是成熟的生命，犹如斟满酒的酒杯。

15

Let me not shame[1] thee, Father,
who displayest thy glory[2] in thy children.

热词天地
1.shame [ʃeɪm] *v.* 使蒙羞；玷污
2.glory ['glɔːrɪ] *n.* 光荣；荣誉

不要让我羞辱您，父亲，
您在您的孩子们身上显出您的荣耀。

16

That love can ever lose is a fact that
we cannot accept as truth.

爱情终将失去，是我们无法当作真理来接
受的一个事实。

流萤集

1

Life's errors cry for the merciful beauty that can modulate their isolation into a harmony with the whole.

生命中的许多错误泪求慈悲之美
以此调节它们的孤独
融入整体使之和谐。

2

They expect thanks for the banished nest
because their cage is shapely and secure.

它们希求感谢那被舍弃的巢居
因为它们的笼子既美观又牢固。

3

Thou hast risen late, my crescent moon,
but my night bird is still awake to greet thee.

我的新月啊,你姗姗来迟,
而我的夜鸟仍等待着向你问候,不曾睡去。

4

The faith waiting in the heart of a seed
promises a miracle of life
which it cannot prove at once.

信念在一粒种子里等待
预示着一个
不能立刻实现的生命奇迹。

5

The two separated shores mingle
their voices
in a song of unfathomed tears.

遥遥相对的两岸在深不可测的泪歌中
融合着他们的声音。

6

As a river in the sea,
work finds its fulfilment
in the depth of leisure.

工作犹如大海中的河川，
在闲适的深海
觅得圆满。

7

The clumsiness of power spoils the key,
and uses the pickaxe.

权力的拙劣宠溺着锁匙，
只好用起了鹤嘴锄。

8

The cloud laughed at the rainbow
saying that it was an upstart
gaudy in its emptiness.
The rainbow calmly answered,
"I am as inevitably real as the sun himself."

云朵嘲笑彩虹,
说它是暴发的新贵,
绚丽的外表下只有空虚。
彩虹平静地回答,
"我无可置疑的真实性就像太阳本身一样。"

9

Birth is from the mystery of night
into the greater mystery of day.

新生是从神秘的黑夜
进入更为神秘的白天。

10

God's world is ever renewed by death,
 a Titan's ever crushed by its own existence.

上帝的世界永远通过死亡再生,
魔界却永远被它自身而粉碎。

11

The breeze whispers to the lotus,
"What is thy secret?"
"It is myself," says the lotus,
"Steal it and I disappear!"

微风对莲花低语道,
"你的秘密是什么?"
"秘密就是我自己,"莲花说,
"偷走它吧,我也会就此消失!"

12

Your calumny against the great is impious,
it hurts yourself;
against the small it is mean,
for it hurts the victim.

你对伟大者的诋毁全无敬意,
它会伤害到你自己;
你对微贱者的诋毁如此卑鄙,
因为它让牺牲者受到伤害。

园丁集 （冰心译）

1

I hold her hands and press her to my breast.

I try to fill my arms with her loveliness, to plunder[1] her sweet smile with kisses, to drink her dark glances with my eyes.

Ah, but, where is it? Who can strain the blue from the sky?

I try to grasp the beauty, it eludes[2] me, leaving only the body in my hands.

Baffled[3] and weary I come back.

How can the body touch the flower which only the spirit may touch?

热词天地

1.plunder ['plʌndə(r)] *vt.* & *vi.* 掠夺；偷；私吞
2.elude [ɪ'luːd] *vt.* 逃避；使……迷惑
3.baffled ['bæfld] *adj.* 带有障板的；阻挡的

我握住她的手把她抱紧在胸前。

我想以她的爱娇来填满我的怀抱,用亲吻来偷劫她的甜笑,用我的眼睛来吸饮她的深黑的一瞥。

啊,但是,它在哪里呢?谁能从天空滤出蔚蓝呢?

我想去把握美;它躲开我,只有躯体留在我的手里。

失望而困乏地,我回来了。

躯体哪能触到那只有精神才能触到的花朵呢?

2

I love you, beloved. Forgive me my love.
Like a bird losing its way I am caught.

When my heart was shaken, it lost its veil[1] and was naked[2]. Cover it with pity, beloved[3], and forgive me my love.

If you cannot love me, beloved, forgive me my pain.
Do not look askance[4] at me from afar[5].
I will steal back to my corner and sit in the dark.
With both hands I will cover my naked shame.
Turn your face from me, beloved, and forgive me my pain.

If you love me, beloved, forgive me my joy.

When my heart is borne away by the flood of happiness, do not smile at my perilous[6] abandonment[7].

When I sit on my throne and rule you with my tyranny of love, when like a goddess I grant you my favour, bear with my pride, beloved, and forgive me my joy.

热词天地

1. veil [veɪl] *n.* 面纱；掩饰
2. naked ['neɪkɪd] *adj.* 裸体的，裸露的
3. beloved [bɪ'lʌvd] *n.* 心爱的人，可爱的人
4. askance [ə'skæns] *adv.* 斜；斜视
5. afar [ə'fɑː(r)] *adv.* 从远处
6. perilous ['perələs] *adj.* 危险的；冒险的
7. abandonment [ə'bændənmənt] *n.* 放弃；抛弃

我爱你,我的爱人,请饶恕我的爱。

像一只迷途的鸟,我被捉住了。

当我的心抖战的时候,它丢了围纱,变成赤裸。用怜悯遮住它吧。爱人,请饶恕我的爱。

如果你不能爱我,爱人,请饶恕我的痛苦。

不要远远地斜视我。

我将偷偷回到我的角落里去,在黑暗中坐地。

我将用双手掩起我赤裸的羞惭。

回过脸去吧,我的爱人,请原谅我的痛苦。

如果你爱我,爱人,请饶恕我的欢乐。

当我的心被快乐的洪水卷走的时候,不要笑我的汹涌的退却。

当我坐在宝座上,用我暴虐的爱来统治你的时候,当我像女神一样向你施恩的时候,饶恕我的骄傲吧,爱人,也饶恕我的快乐。

新月集

The Beginning

"Where have I come from, where did you pick me up?" the baby asked its mother.

She answered half crying, half laughing, and clasping the baby to her breast,—"You were hidden in my heart as its desire, my darling.

You were in the dolls of my childhood's games; and when with clay[1] I made the image of my god every morning, I made and unmade you then.

You were enshrined with our household deity, in his worship I worshipped you.

In all my hopes and my loves, in my life, in the life of my mother you have lived.

In the lap[2] of the deathless Spirit who rules our home you have been nursed for ages.

When in girlhood my heart was opening its petals, you hovered[3] as a fragrance about it.

Your tender softness bloomed in my youthful limbs[4], like a glow in the sky before the sunrise.

Heaven's first darling, twin-born with the morning light, you have floated down the stream of the world's life, and at last you have stranded[5] on my heart.

As I gaze on your face, mystery overwhelms me; you who belong to all have become mine.

For fear of losing you I hold you tight to my breast. What magic has snared the world's treasure in these slender arms of mine?"

热词天地
1.clay [kleɪ] n. 黏土，泥土
2.lap [læp] vt. 折叠；包裹，缠绕
3.hover ['hɒvə(r)] vi. 盘旋；徘徊；犹豫
4.limb [lɪm] n. 肢，翼
5.strand [strænd] n.（绳子的）股，绞

开始

"我从哪里来,你从哪儿捡到的我?"孩子问母亲。

她把孩子紧紧地搂在胸前,哭笑不得地答道:

"你曾是我藏在心底的心愿,我的宝贝。

"你曾存在我儿时玩的娃娃身上;每天早晨我用泥土捏出我的神像,我捏来捏去的就是你。

"你曾和家庭守护神一同被供奉,我敬拜家神时也敬拜了你。

"你曾活在我所有的希望和爱情里,在我的生命里,在我母亲的生命里。

"你曾在掌管我们家那不死精灵的膝上,已经被抚育了好多年。

"女孩时的我,内心如花瓣儿张开,你就像一缕花香萦绕其中。

"你的温柔在我年轻的肢体上开了花,犹如日出前天空的一道曙光。

"上天的第一宠儿,晨曦的好兄弟,你沿着世界生命之溪顺流而下,终于停泊在我的心头。

"每当凝视你的小脸,神秘感席卷而来;原本属于一切的你,现今竟成了我的。

"我将你牢牢地搂在胸前,生怕失去。是什么魔法把这世界最珍贵的宝贝交托于我纤弱的臂弯里呢?"

Vocation

When the gong sounds ten in the morning and I walk to school by our lane[1],

Every day I meet the hawker[2] crying, "Bangles, crystal bangles!"

There is nothing to hurry him on, there is no road he must take, no place he must go to, no time when he must come home.

I wish I were a hawker, spending my day in the road, crying, "Bangles, crystal bangles!"

When at four in the afternoon I come back from the school,

I can see through the gate of that house the gardener digging the ground.

He does what he likes with his spade, he soils his clothes with dust, nobody takes him to task if he gets baked in the sun or gets wet.

I wish I were a gardener digging away at the garden with nobody to stop me from digging.

Just as it gets dark in the evening and my mother sends me to bed,

I can see through my open window the watchman walking up and down.

The lane is dark and lonely, and the street-lamp stands like a giant with one red eye in its head.

The watchman swings his lantern and walks with his shadow at his side, and never once goes to bed in his life.

I wish I were a watchman walking the streets all night, chasing the shadows with my lantern.

热词天地

1. lane [leɪn] *n.* 小路,小巷;航道
2. hawker [ˈhɔːkə(r)] *n.* 沿街叫卖者

职业

晨钟在十点敲响的时候,我沿着我们的小巷到学校去。

我每天都会碰见的那个小贩吆喝着:"手镯咯,亮晶晶的手镯!"

他没有什么要紧的事,没有必须要走的街道,没有什么他一定要去的地方,也没有回家的固定时间点。

我希望我是一个小贩,在街上过日子,吆喝着:"镯子咯,亮晶晶的镯子!"

下午四点,我从学校回家,

从一户人家的院门,我可以看到一个园丁在掘地。

他举着锄头随意地掘地,他的衣服被泥土染脏,他被太阳晒黑或身上被打湿,都没人责骂他。

我希望我是一个在花园里掘地的园丁,没有人来阻拦。

天色刚黑,妈妈就送我上床。

透过敞开的窗户,我能看见更夫来回逡巡。

幽黑又冷清的小巷里,路灯孑然独立,犹如头上生着红色独眼的巨人。

更夫摇晃着他的提灯,随同身边的影子一同前行,他的一生从未有过上床休息的时刻。

我希望我是一个更夫,在街上整夜游荡,提着灯追逐影子。

Baby's Way

If baby only wanted to, he could fly up to heaven this moment.

It is not for nothing that he does not leave us.

He loves to rest his head on mother's bosom, and cannot ever bear to lose sight of her.

Baby knows all manner of wise words, though few on earth can understand their meaning.

It is not for nothing that he never wants to speak.

The one thing he wants is to learn mother's words from mother's lips. That is why he looks so innocent.

Baby had a heap of gold and pearls, yet he came like a beggar on to this earth.

It is not for nothing he came in such a disguise.

This dear little naked mendicant[1] pretends to be utterly helpless, so that he may beg for mother's wealth of love.

Baby was so free from every tie in the land of the tiny crescent[2] moon.

It was not for nothing he gave up his freedom.

He knows that there is room for endless joy in mother's little corner of a heart, and it is sweeter far than liberty to be caught and pressed in her dear arms.

Baby never knew how to cry. He dwelt in the land of perfect bliss.

It is not for nothing he has chosen to shed tears.

Though with the smile of his dear face he draws mother's yearning heart to him, yet his little cries over tiny troubles weave the double bond of pity and love.

热词天地

1.mendicant ['mendɪkənt] *adj.* 行乞的
2.crescent ['kresnt] *n.* 新月；月牙
　rest on 搁在 / 支撑在……上；依赖于
　on earth 究竟，到底
　a heap of 一大堆，很多，大量
　pretend to be 假充；冒充
　beg for 乞讨（食物、钱等）；恳求，乞求

孩童之道

假如孩子愿意,他可以此刻飞上云霄。
他之所以不离开我们,并非毫无缘由。
他喜欢把头倚在母亲的怀里,不能忍受母亲在视线中消失。
孩子了解各种各样的聪明话,尽管世间很少有人深明其意。
他之所以永远不想说话,并非毫无缘由。
他最想做的一件事,就是学习母亲吐露的语言,因此他看上去如此天真无邪。
孩子拥有成堆的金银财宝,然而他却像个乞丐一样降临人世。
他之所以带着这样的伪装而来,并非毫无缘由。
这个光着屁股的小乞丐,假装成无辜的样子,从而能更好地向母亲乞求更多的爱。
孩子在纤小的新月世界里,无拘无束。
他之所以放弃了自由,并非毫无缘由。
他知道有无穷的快乐藏在妈妈心中小小一隅,被妈妈爱的手臂拥抱,那甜美远胜自由。
孩子可以永远都不了解哭泣,他生活在一片乐土里。
他之所以流泪,并非毫无缘由。
尽管他用小脸蛋上可爱的微笑吸引了母亲渴望的心,可是,他因为细微麻烦而引发的小小哭声,却编织成了怜与爱的双重牵绊。

The Judge

Say of him what you please, but I know my child's failings. I do not love him because he is good, but because he is my little child.

How should you know how dear he can be when you try to weigh his merits[1] against his faults?

When I must punish him he becomes all the more a part of my being.

When I cause his tears to come my heart weeps with him.

I alone have a right to blame and punish, for he only may chastise[2] who loves.

热词天地

1.merit ['merɪt] *n.* 价值；优点
2.chastise [tʃæ'staɪz] *vt.* 严惩（某人）
　weigh against 与之相当

审判官

你可以对他畅所欲言,然而我了解我孩子的弱点。
我爱他并非因为他多优秀,只是因为他是我的小宝贝。
若你将他的优缺点加以衡量,也许就明白他是如此可爱。
当我必须惩罚他的时候,他更加成为我生命的一部分了。
当我惹他泪水涟涟时,我的心也同他一起哭泣。
只有我才有权去责骂和惩罚他,因为只有深爱的人才可以惩戒他。

开始

吉檀迦利 （冰心 译）

Innocence

When my play was with thee I never questioned who thou wert. I knew nor shyness nor fear, my life was boisterous[1].

In the early morning thou wouldst call me from my sleep like my own comrade and lead me running from glade to glade[2].

On those days I never cared to know the meaning of songs thou sangest to me. Only my voice took up the tunes, and my heart danced in their cadence[3].

Now, when the playtime is over, what is this sudden sight that is come upon me? The world with eyes bent upon thy feet stands in awe[4] with all its silent stars.

热词天地

1. boisterous ['bɔɪstərəs] *adj.* 狂暴的；喧闹的；骚嚷的
2. glade [gleɪd] *n.* 林中空地
3. cadence ['keɪdns] *n.* （声音的）抑扬顿挫
4. awe [ɔː] *n.* 敬畏；惊惧；惊叹

无知

当我是同你做游戏的时候,我从来没有问过你是谁。我不懂得羞怯和惧怕,我的生活是热闹的。

清晨你就来把我唤醒,像我自己的伙伴一样,带着我跑过林野。

那些日子,我从来不想去了解你对我唱的歌曲的意义。我只随声附和,我的心应节跳舞。

现在,游戏的时光已过,这突然来到我眼前的情景是什么呢?世界低下眼来看着你的双脚,和它的肃静的众星一同敬畏地站着。

Thy Voice

If thou speakest not I will fill my heart with thy silence and endure it. I will keep still and wait like the night with starry vigil and its head bent low with patience.

The morning will surely come, the darkness will vanish, and thy voice pour down in golden streams breaking through the sky.

Then thy words will take wing in songs from every one of my birds nests, and thy melodies will break forth in flowers in all my forest groves.

你的声音

若是你不说话,我就含忍着,以你的沉默来填满我的心。我要沉静地等候,像黑夜在星空中无眠,忍耐地低首。

清晨一定会来,黑暗也要消隐,你的声音将划破天空从金泉中下注。

那时你的话语,要在我的每一鸟巢中生翼发声,你的音乐,要在我林丛繁花中盛开绽放。

The Wayside Where Shadow Chases Light

This is my delight, thus to wait and watch at the wayside where shadow chases[1] light and the rain comes in the wake of the summer.

Messengers, with tidings from unknown skies, greet me and speed along the road. My heart is glad within, and the breath of the passing breeze is sweet.

From dawn till dusk I sit here before my door, and I know that of a sudden the happy moment will arrive when I shall see.

In the meanwhile I smile and I sing all alone. In the meanwhile the air is filling with the perfume[2] of promise.

热词天地

1. chase [tʃeɪs] *vt.* 追捕；追求
2. perfume ['pɜ:fju:m] *n.* 香水；香料
   in the wake of 尾随，紧跟，仿效；随着

影逐光的地方

在光影追逐的地方,在雨至初醒的夏日,驻足路旁静待观望,这令我快乐。

带着消息从天而降的信使们,匆忙地向我致意,继而沿着路疾驰离去。我万分欣喜,呼吸着清风都倍感甜蜜。

我坐在门前守着,自黎明至黄昏。因为我知道只要见到你,那惊喜的幸福时刻便会降临。

同时,我会始终含笑而歌,空气里也充溢着承诺的香气。

Your Pour

Thou hast made me endless, such is thy pleasure. This frail vessel thou emptiest again and again, and fillest it ever with fresh life.

This little flute of a reed thou hast carried over hills and dales, and hast breathed through it melodies eternally new.

At the immortal touch of thy hands my little heart loses its limits in joy and gives birth to utterance ineffable.

Thy infinite gifts come to me only on these very small hands of mine. Ages pass, and still thou pourest, and still there is room to fill.

你的倾注

你已经使我永生,这样做是你的欢乐。这脆薄的杯儿,你不断的把它倒空,又不断的以新生命来充满。

这小小的苇笛,你携带着它逾山越谷,从笛管里吹出永新的音乐。

在你双手的不朽的安抚下,我的小小的心,消融在无边快乐之中,发出不可言说的词调。

你的无穷的赐予只倾入我小小的手中。时代过去了,你还在倾注,而我的手里还有余量待充满。

Drunk with the Joy of Singing

When thou commandest me to sing it seems that my heart would break with pride; and I look to thy face, and tears come to my eyes.

All that is harsh and dissonant in my life melts into one sweet harmony—and my adoration spreads wings like a glad bird on its flight across the sea.

I know thou takest pleasure in my singing. I know that only as a singer I come before thy presence.

I touch by the edge of the far-spreading wing of my song thy feet which I could never aspire to reach.

Drunk with the joy of singing I forget myself and call thee friend who art my lord.

在歌唱中陶醉

当你命令我歌唱的时候,我的心似乎要因着骄傲而炸裂;我仰望着你的脸,眼泪涌上我的眶里。

我生命中一切的凝涩与矛盾融化成一片甜柔的谐音——我的赞颂像一只欢乐的鸟,振翼飞越海洋。

我知道你欢喜我的歌唱。我知道只因为我是个歌者,才能走到你的面前。

我用我的歌曲的远伸的翅梢,触到了你的双脚,那是我从来不敢想望触到的。

在歌唱中陶醉,我忘了自己,你本是我的主人,我却称你为朋友。

My Heart Longs to Join in Thy Song

I know not how thou singest, my master! I ever listen in silent amazement.

The light of thy music illumines the world. The life breath of thy music runs from sky to sky. The holy stream of thy music breaks through all stony obstacles and rushes on.

My heart longs to join in thy song, but vainly struggles for a voice. I would speak, but speech breaks not into song, and I cry out baffled. Ah, thou hast made my heart captive in the endless meshes of thy music, my master!

我的心渴望与你合唱

　　我不知道你怎样地唱，我的主人！我总在惊奇地静听。

　　你的音乐的光辉照亮了世界。你的音乐的气息透彻诸天。你的音乐的圣泉冲过一切阻挡的岩石，向前奔涌。

　　我的心渴望和你合唱，而挣扎不出一点声音。我想说话，但是言语不成歌曲，我叫不出来。呵，你使我的心变成了你的音乐的漫天大网中的俘虏，我的主人！

Come Out of Thy Meditations

Leave this chanting and singing and telling of beads! Whom dost thou worship in this lonely dark corner of a temple with doors all shut? Open thine eyes and see thy God is not before thee!

He is there where the tiller is tilling the hard ground and where the pathmaker is breaking stones. He is with them in sun and in shower, and his garment is covered with dust. Put of thy holy mantle and even like him come down on the dusty soil!

Deliverance? Where is this deliverance to be found? Our master himself has joyfully taken upon him the bonds of creation; he is bound with us all for ever.

Come out of thy meditations and leave aside thy flowers and incense! What harm is there if thy clothes become tattered and stained? Meet him and stand by him in toil and in sweat of thy brow.

从静坐中走出来罢

把礼赞和数珠撇在一边罢!你在门窗紧闭幽暗孤寂的殿角里,向谁礼拜呢?睁开眼你看,上帝不在你的面前!

他是在锄着枯地的农夫那里,在敲石的造路工人那里。太阳下,阴雨里,他和他们同在,衣袍上蒙着尘土。脱掉你的圣袍,甚至像他一样的下到泥土里去罢!

超脱吗?从哪里找超脱呢?我们的主已经高高兴兴地把创造的锁链带起;他和我们大家永远连系在一起。

从静坐里走出来罢,丢开供养的香花!你的衣服污损了又何妨呢?去迎接他,在劳动里、流汗里,和他站在一起罢。

Light, Oh Where Is the Light?

Light, oh where is the light? Kindle it with the burning fire of desire!

There is the lamp but never a flicker of a flame—is such thy fate, my heart? Ah, death were better by far for thee!

Misery knocks at thy door, and her message is that thy lord is wakeful, and he calls thee to the love-tryst through the darkness of night.

The sky is overcast with clouds and the rain is ceaseless. I know not what this is that stirs in me—I know not its meaning.

A moment's flash of lightning drags down a deeper gloom on my sight, and my heart gropes for the path to where the music of the night calls me.

Light, oh where is the light? Kindle it with the burning fire of desire! It thunders and the wind rushes screaming through the void. The night is black as a black stone. Let not the hours pass by in the dark. Kindle the lamp of love with thy life.

灯火,灯火在哪里呢?

灯火,灯火在哪里呢?用熊熊的渴望之火把它点上罢!

灯在这里,却没有一丝火焰,——这是你的命运吗,我的心呵!你还不如死了好!

悲哀在你门上敲着,她传话说你的主醒着呢,他叫你在夜的黑暗中奔赴爱的约会。

云雾遮满天空,雨也不停地下。我不知道我心里有什么在动荡,——我不懂得它的意义。

一霎的电光,在我的视线上抛下一道更深的黑暗,我的心摸索着寻找那夜的音乐对我呼唤的径路。

灯火,灯火在哪里呢?用熊熊的渴望之火把它点上罢!雷声在响,狂风怒吼着穿过天空。夜像黑岩一般的黑。不要让时间在黑暗中度过罢。用你的生命把爱的灯点上罢。

开始 55

Where Dost Thou Stand Behind Them All

Where dost thou stand behind them all, my lover, hiding thyself in the shadows? They push thee and pass thee by on the dusty road, taking thee for naught. I wait here weary hours spreading my offerings for thee, while passers-by come and take my flowers, one by one, and my basket is nearly empty.

The morning time is past, and the noon. In the shade of evening my eyes are drowsy with sleep. Men going home glance at me and smile and fill me with shame. I sit like a beggar maid, drawing my skirt over my face, and when they ask me, what it is I want, I drop my eyes and answer them not.

Oh, how, indeed, could I tell them that for thee I wait, and that thou hast promised to come. How could I utter for shame that I keep for my dowry this poverty. Ah, I hug this pride in the secret of my heart.

I sit on the grass and gaze upon the sky and dream of the sudden splendour of thy coming—all the lights ablaze, golden pennons flying over thy car, and they at the roadside standing agape, when they see thee come down from thy seat to raise me from the dust, and set at thy side this ragged beggar girl a-tremble with shame and pride, like a creeper in a summer breeze.

But time glides on and still no sound of the wheels of thy chariot. Many a procession passes by with noise and shouts and glamour of glory.

Is it only thou who wouldst stand in the shadow silent and behind them all?

And only I who would wait and weep and wear out my heart in vain longing?

你站在大家背后

我的情人,你站在大家背后,藏在何处的阴影中呢?在尘土飞扬的道上,他们把你推开走过,没有理睬你。在乏倦的时间,我摆开礼品来等候你,过路的人把我的香花一朵一朵的拿去,我的花篮几乎空了。

清晨,中午都过去了。暮色中,我倦眼朦胧。回家的人们瞟着我微笑,使我满心羞惭。我像女丐一般地坐着,拉起裙儿盖上脸,当他们问我要什么的时候,我垂目没有答应。

呵,真的,我怎能告诉他们说我是在等候你,而且你也应许说你一定会来。我又怎能抱愧地说我的妆奁就是贫穷。呵,我在我心的微隐处紧抱着这一段骄荣。

我坐在草地上凝望天空,梦想着你来临时候那忽然炫耀的豪华——万彩交辉,车辇上金旗飞扬,在道旁众目睽睽之下,你从车座下降,把我从尘埃中扶起坐在你的旁边,这褴褛的丐女,含羞带喜,像蔓藤在暴风中颤摇。

但是时间流过了,还听不见你的车辇的轮声。许多仪仗队伍都在光彩喧闹中走过了。
你只要静默地站在他们背后吗?
我只能哭泣着等待,把我的心折磨在空虚的伫望之中吗?

He Comes, Comes

Have you not heard his silent steps? He comes, comes, ever comes.

Every moment and every age, every day and every night he comes, comes, ever comes.

Many a song have I sung in many a mood of mind, but all their notes have always proclaimed, "He comes, comes, ever comes."

In the fragrant days of sunny April through the forest path he comes, comes, ever comes.

In the rainy gloom of July nights on the thundering chariot of clouds he comes, comes, ever comes.

In sorrow after sorrow it is his steps that press upon my heart, and it is the golden touch of his feet that makes my joy to shine.

他正在走来,走来

你没有听见他静悄的脚步吗?他正在走来,走来,一直不停地走来。

每一个时间,每一个年代,每日每夜,他总在走来,走来,一直不停地走来。

在许多不同的心情里,我唱过许多歌曲,但在这些歌调里,我总在宣告说:"他正在走来,走来,一直不停地走来。"

四月芬芳的晴天里,他从林径中走来,走来,一直不停地走来。

七月阴暗的雨夜中,他坐着隆隆的云辇,走来,走来,一直不停地走来。

愁闷相继之中,是他的脚步踏在我的心上,是他的双脚的黄金般的接触,使我的快乐发出光辉。

开始

Beautiful Is Thy Wristlet

Beautiful is thy wristlet, decked with stars and cunningly wrought in myriad-coloured jewels. But more beautiful to me thy sword with its curve of lightning like the outspread wings of the divine bird of Vishnu, perfectly poised in the angry red light of the sunset.

It quivers like the one last response of life in ecstasy of pain at the final stroke of death; it shines like the pure flame of being burning up earthly sense with one fierce flash.

Beautiful is thy wristlet, decked with starry gems; but thy sword, O lord of thunder, is wrought with uttermost beauty, terrible to behold or think of.

你的手镯真是美丽

你的手镯真是美丽,镶着星辰,精巧地嵌着五光十色的珠宝。但是依我看来你的宝剑是更美的,那弯弯的闪光像毗湿奴的神鸟展开的翅翼,完美地平悬在落日怒发的红光里。

它颤抖着像生命受死亡的最后一击时,在痛苦的昏迷中的最后反应;它炫耀着像将烬的世情的纯焰,最后猛烈的一闪。

你的手镯真是美丽,镶着星辰般的珠宝;但是你的宝剑,呵,雷霆的主,是铸得绝顶美丽,看到想到都是可畏的。

开始

A Kingly Jest

I had gone a-begging from door to door in the village path, when thy golden chariot appeared in the distance like a gorgeous dream and I wondered who was this King of all kings!

My hopes rose high and methought my evil days were at an end, and I stood waiting for alms to be given unasked and for wealth scattered on all sides in the dust.

The chariot stopped where I stood. Thy glance fell on me and thou camest down with a smile. I felt that the luck of my life had come at last. Then of a sudden thou didst hold out thy right hand and say "What hast thou to give to me?"

Ah, what a kingly jest was it to open thy palm to a beggar to beg! I was confused and stood undecided, and then from my wallet I slowly took out the least little grain of corn and gave it to thee.

But how great my surprise when at the day's end I emptied my bag on the floor to find a least little gram of gold among the poor heap. I bitterly wept and wished that I had had the heart to give thee my all.

一个天大的玩笑

我在村路上沿门求乞的时候,你的金辇像一个华丽的梦从远处出现,我在猜想这位万王之王是谁!

我的希望高升,我觉得我苦难的日子将要告终,我站着等候你自动的施与,等待那散掷在尘埃里的财宝。

车辇在我站立的地方停住了。你看到我,微笑着下车。我觉得我的运气到底来了。忽然你伸出右手来说:"你有什么给我呢?"

呵,这开的是什么样的帝王的玩笑,向一个乞丐伸手求乞!我糊涂了,犹疑地站着,然后从我的口袋里慢慢地拿出一粒最小的玉米献上给你。

但是我一惊不小,当我在晚上把口袋倒在地上的时候,在我乞讨来的粗劣东西之中,我发现了一粒金子。我痛哭了,恨我没有慷慨地将我所有都献给你。

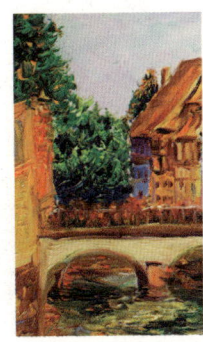

It Is Time to Sit Quite

I ask for a moment's indulgence to sit by thy side. The works that I have in hand I will finish afterwards.

Away from the sight of thy face my heart knows no rest nor respite, and my work becomes an endless toil in a shoreless sea of toil.

Today the summer has come at my window with its sighs and murmurs; and the bees are plying their minstrelsy at the court of the flowering grove.

Now it is time to sit quite, face to face with thee, and to sing dedication of live in this silent and overflowing leisure.

静坐的时光

请容我懈怠一会儿,来坐在你的身旁。我手边的工作等一下子再去完成。

不在你的面前,我的心就不知道什么是安逸和休息,我的工作变成了无边的劳役海中的无尽的劳役。

今天,炎暑来到我的窗前,轻嘘微语:群蜂在花树的宫廷中尽情弹唱。

这正是应该静坐的时光,和你相对,在这静寂和无边的闲暇里唱出生命的献歌。

When I Try to Bow to Thee

Here is thy footstool and there rest thy feet where live the poorest, and lowliest, and lost.

When I try to bow to thee, my obeisance cannot reach down to the depth where thy feet rest among the poorest, and lowliest, and lost.

Pride can never approach to where thou walkest in the clothes of the humble among the poorest, and lowliest, and lost.

My heart can never find its way to where thou keepest company with the companionless among the poorest, the lowliest, and the lost.

我想向你鞠躬

这是你的脚凳,你在最贫最贱最失所的人群中歇足。

我想向你鞠躬,我的敬礼不能达到你歇足地方的深处——那最贫最贱最失所的人群中。

你穿着破敝的衣服,在最贫最贱最失所的人群中行走,骄傲永远不能走近这个地方。

你和那最没有朋友的最贫最贱最失所的人们作伴,我的心永远找不到那个地方。

I Kept Her in My Heart

She who ever had remained in the depth of my being, in the twilight of gleams and of glimpses; she who never opened her veils in the morning light, will be my last gift to thee, my God, folded in my final song.

Words have wooed yet failed to win her; persuasion has stretched to her its eager arms in vain.

I have roamed from country to country keeping her in the core of my heart, and around her have risen and fallen the growth and decay of my life.

Over my thoughts and actions, my slumbers and dreams, she reigned yet dwelled alone and apart.

Many a man knocked at my door and asked for her and turned away in despair.

There was none in the world who ever saw her face to face, and she remained in her loneliness waiting for thy recognition.

我将她深藏于心

那在神光离合之中,潜藏在我生命深处的她;那在晨光中永远不肯揭开面纱的她,我的上帝,我要用最后的一首歌把她包裹起来,作为我给你的最后的献礼。

无数求爱的话,都已说过,但还没有赢得她的心;劝诱向她伸出渴望的臂,也是枉然。

我把她深藏在心里,到处漫游,我生命的荣枯围绕着她起落。
她统治着我的思想、行动和睡梦,她却自己独居索处。

许多的人叩我的门来访问她,都失望地回去。

在这世界上从没有人和她面对过,她在孤守着静待你的赏识。

I Am Here to Sing thee Songs

I am here to sing thee songs. In this hall of thine I have a corner seat.

In thy world I have no work to do; my useless life can only break out in tunes without a purpose.

When the hour strikes for thy silent worship at the dark temple of midnight, command me, my master, to stand before thee to sing.

When in the morning air the golden harp is tuned, honour me, commanding my presence.

我来为你唱歌

我来为你唱歌。在你的厅堂中,我坐在屋角。

在你的世界中我无事可做;我无用的生命只能放出无目的的歌声。

在你黑暗的殿中,夜半敲起默祷的钟声的时候,命令我罢,我的主人,来站在你面前歌唱。

当金琴在晨光中调好的时候,宠赐我罢,命令我来到你的面前。

It Is Only for Thee That I Hope

Clouds heap upon clouds and it darkens. Ah, love, why dost thou let me wait outside at the door all alone?

In the busy moments of the noontide work I am with the crowd, but on this dark lonely day it is only for thee that I hope.

If thou showest me not thy face, if thou leavest me wholly aside, I know not how I am to pass these long, rainy hours.

I keep gazing on the far-away gloom of the sky, and my heart wanders wailing with the restless wind.

我只企望你

　　云霾堆积,黑暗渐深。呵,爱,你为什么让我独自在门外等候?

　　在中午工作最忙的时候,我和大家在一起,但在这黑暗寂寞的日子,我只企望着你。

　　若是你不容我见面,若是你完全把我抛弃,我真不知将如何度过这悠长的雨天。

　　我不住地凝望遥远的阴空,我的心和不宁的风一同彷徨悲叹。

第二卷
迷失的星星

飞鸟集

1

What language is thine, O sea?
The language of eternal¹ question.
What language is thy answer, O sky?
The language of eternal silence.

热词天地

1. eternal [ɪ'tɜ:nl] *adj.* 永恒的，永久的

海水呀，你讲的是什么？
是永恒的疑问。
天空呀，你回答的是什么？
是永恒的沉默。

2

It is the tears of the earth that keep
here smiles in bloom.

是大地的泪水,
使她的微笑保持青春不谢。

3

The waterfall[1] sing, "I find my song,
when I find my freedom."

热词天地

1.waterfall ['wɔ:təfɔ:l] *n.* 瀑布;瀑布似的东西

瀑布歌唱道:"我寻到自由时便有了歌声了。"

迷失的星星　79

4

The stars are not afraid to appear[1] like fireflies.

热词天地

1.appear [ə'pɪə(r)] *vi.* 出现；显现

群星不怕像萤火那样出现。

5

The sparrow[1] is sorry for the peacock at the burden[2] of its tail.

热词天地

1.sparrow ['spærəʊ] *n.* 麻雀
2.burden ['bɜːdn] *n.* 负担，包袱；责任，义务

麻雀为孔雀驮着它的尾羽而替它担忧。

6

The fish in the water is silent, the animal on the earth is noisy, the bird in the air is singing.

But Man has in him the silence of the sea, the noise of the earth and the music of the air.

水里的鱼儿是沉默的,
陆地上的兽类是喧闹的,
空中的鸟儿是歌唱的。
但是,人类却融合了海里的沉默、
陆地的喧闹和空中的音乐。

7

Bees sip[1] honey from flowers and hum[2] their thanks when they leave.

The gaudy[3] butterfly is sure that the flowers owe thanks to him.

热词天地

1. sip [sɪp] *n.* 呷的动作
2. hum [hʌm] *vt.* 哼唱
3. gaudy ['gɔːdɪ] *adj.* 花哨的；俗气的
   owe to 欠……；应该感谢，把……归功于

蜜蜂从花中采蜜，离开时嗡嗡致谢。
浮华的蝴蝶却确信花儿应当向它道谢。

8

The woodcutter's axe begged for its handle from the tree.
The tree gave it.

樵夫的斧头向树要斧柄。
树便给了他。

9

God's great power is in the gentle breeze,
not in the storm.

上帝的巨大力量是在和风中，
而非暴风骤雨里。

10

The cobweb[1] pretends to catch dewdrops[2] and catches flies.

热词天地
1.cobweb ['kɒbweb] *n.* 蜘蛛网
2.dewdrop ['djuːdrɒp] *n.* 露珠；露滴

蛛网假装捕捉露珠，却捉住了苍蝇。

11

The pet dog suspects the universe for scheming[1] to take its place.

热词天地
1.scheme [skiːm] *vi.* & *vt.* 策划，图谋

宠物狗疑心宇宙图谋取代它的位置。

12

The best does not come alone.
It comes with the company[1] of the all.

热词天地

1. company ['kʌmpənɪ] *n.* 公司；商号

最好的东西不是独来的，
它伴随着所有东西而来。

13

"How may I sing to thee and worship, O sun?" asked the little flower.
"By the simple silence of thy purity," answered the sun.

"太阳啊,我该怎样歌唱来表达对你的崇敬呢?"小花问。
"用你那纯洁而朴实的沉默就足矣。"太阳回答。

14

Man is worse than an animal when he is an animal.

当人类变成野兽时,会比野兽更为糟糕。

15

The service of the fruit is precious,
the service of the flower is sweet,
but let my service be the service of the leaves
in its shade of humble[1] devotion[2].

热词天地

1. humble ['hʌmbl] *adj.* 谦逊的；简陋的
2. devotion [dɪ'vəʊʃn] *n.* 献身，奉献；忠诚

果实的服务是宝贵的，
花儿的服务是甜蜜的；
但让我像绿叶一样服务吧，
谦卑地奉献绿荫！

流萤集

1

A light laughter in the steps of creation
carries it swiftly across time.

在造物主脚步里一声轻笑，
迅速地将其穿越时光之河。

2

The shore whispers to the sea:
"Write to me what thy waves struggle to say."
The sea writes in foam again and again
and wipes off the lines in a boisterous despair.

海岸对大海低语：
"你的波涛拼命地要说什么，写给我吧。"
大海蘸着浮沫反复书写，
又在喧嚷的绝望中，擦去了字句行行。

3

One who was distant came near to me in the morning,
and still nearer when taken away by night.

离我遥远得人在清晨向我走近，
当他被黑夜带走时依然向我走近。

迷失的星星

4

There smiles the Divine Child
among his playthings of unmeaning clouds
and ephemeral lights and shadows.

那圣洁的孩子在微笑着,
在他与那无意义的云朵和瞬变的光影
游戏的时候。

5

Let me not grope in vain in the dark
but keep my mind still in the faith
that the day will break
and truth will appear in its simplicity.

我不要在黑暗里徒然探索
却是要保持头脑冷静并始终坚信
长夜必将破晓,
真理必将显现在它的简朴里。

6

God seeks comrades and claims love,
the Devil seeks slaves and claims obedience.

上帝寻找伙伴，要求的是爱慕；
魔鬼寻找奴隶，要求的是服从。

7

The soil in return for her service
keeps the tree tied to her,
the sky asks nothing and leaves it free.

土地将树木捆绑在身上
以此作为她服务的回报，
天空却别无所求，放它自由。

8

Jewel—like the immortal
does not boast of its length of years
but of the scintillating point of its moment.

宝石——如同不朽者，
不会炫耀其岁月漫漫，
而是自豪其顷刻间的璀璨。

9

The child ever dwells in the mystery of ageless time,
unobscured by the dust of history.

孩童永驻于永恒时光的秘境，
历史的尘埃无法将其蒙昧。

10

Thy shy little pomegranate bud,
blushing to-day behind her veil,
will burst into a passionate flower
to-morrow when I am away.

你这个小小的羞涩的石榴花蕾,
在面纱的后面羞红了脸,
明天我要离开时,
却会盛放为一朵热情之花。

采果集

1

Be ready to launch forth, my heart! and let those linger[1] who must.

For your name has been called in the morning sky.

Wait for none!

The desire of the bud[2] is for the night and dew, but the blown flower cries for the freedom of light.

Burst your sheath[3], my heart, and come forth!

热词天地

1.linger ['lɪŋgə(r)] *vi.* 逗留，徘徊；缓慢消失
2.bud [bʌd] *n.* 芽，萌芽
3.sheath [ʃi:θ] *n.* 护套；鞘
　be ready to 预备，即将，乐意
　come forth 出现，涌现

准备启程吧,我的心!让那些徘徊的去徘徊吧。

因为清晨的天空,有你的名字在回响。

不用再等待!

蓓蕾企盼的是黑夜与露珠,盛开的花朵渴望的是光明里的自由。

冲破你的襁褓吧,我的心啊,出来吧!

2

When I lingered among my hoarded treasure I felt like a worm that feeds in the dark upon the fruit where it was born.

I leave this prison of decay[1].

I care not to haunt[2] the mouldy[3] stillness, for I go in search of everlasting youth; I throw away all that is not one with my life nor as light as my laughter.

I run through time and, O my heart, in your chariot[4] dances the poet who sings while he wanders.

热词天地

1. decay [dɪ'keɪ] *vt.* & *vi.* （使）腐烂；腐朽
2. haunt [hɔːnt] *vt.* 时常萦绕心头；使困窘
3. mouldy ['məʊldɪ] *adj.* 发霉的；破旧的
4. chariot ['tʃærɪət] *n.* 敞篷双轮马车（古代用于战争或竞赛）；战车
   in search of 寻找

每当徘徊于收藏的财富之间时,我就觉得自己像一条蛀虫,在黑暗中噬咬着滋生自己的果实。

我离开这座腐坏的牢狱。

我不愿依附在这腐烂的沉寂里,我要去寻找那永驻的青春;一切与我生命无关的,一切不似我笑声轻盈的,全都要抛却。

我在时间里穿梭,哦,我的心,行吟诗人在你的战车里起舞。

园丁集 （冰心 译）

1

Why did the lamp go out?

I shaded it with my cloak to save it from the wind, that is why the lamp went out.

Why did the flower fade[1]?

I pressed it to my heart with anxious[2] love, that is why the flower faded.

Why did the stream dry up?

I put a dam across it to have it for my use, that is why the stream dried up.

Why did the harp-string break?

I tried to force a note that was beyond its power, that is why the harp-string is broken.

热词天地

1. shade [ʃeɪd] *vt.* 遮蔽；险胜
2. anxious [ˈæŋkʃəs] *adj.* 焦急的；渴望的
   save from 从……中救出；使免受
   dry up 枯竭；（使……）干涸

灯为什么熄了呢?
我用斗篷遮住它怕它被风吹灭,因此灯熄了。
花为什么谢了呢?
我的热恋的爱把它紧压在我的心上,因此花谢了。
泉为什么干了呢?
我盖起一道堤把它拦起给我使用,因此泉干了。
琴弦为什么断了呢?
我强弹一个它力不能胜的音节,因此琴弦断了。

2

I often wonder where lie hidden the boundaries[1] of recognition between man and the beast whose heart knows no spoken language.

Through what primal paradise in a remote morning of creation ran the simple path by which their hearts visited each other.

Those marks of their constant tread[2] have not been effaced[3] though their kinship has been long forgotten.

Yet suddenly in some wordless music the dim memory wakes up and the beast gazes into the man's face with a tender trust, and the man looks down into its eyes with amused affection.

It seems that the two friends meet masked and vaguely know each other through the disguise[4].

热词天地

1. boundary ['baʊndrɪ] *n.* 分界线；范围
2. tread [tred] *vt.* 踩；踏
3. efface [ɪ'feɪs] *vt.* 擦掉；抹去
4. disguise [dɪs'gaɪz] *vt.* 隐瞒；掩饰

我常常思索，人和动物之间没有语言，他们心中互相认识的界线在哪里。

在远古创世的清晨，通过哪一条太初乐园的单纯的小径，他们的心曾彼此访问过。

他们的亲属关系早被忘却，他们不变的足印的符号并没有消灭。

可是忽然在那无言的音乐中，那模糊的记忆清醒起来，动物用温柔的信任注视着人的脸，人也用嬉笑的感情下望着它的眼睛。

好像两个朋友戴着面具相逢，在伪装下彼此模糊地互认着。

吉檀迦利 （冰心 译）

Lost Star

When the creation was new and all the stars shone in their first splendour[1], the gods held their assembly[2] in the sky and sang "Oh, the picture of perfection! the joy unalloyed!"

But one cried of a sudden—"It seems that somewhere there is a break in the chain of light and one of the stars has been lost."

The golden string of their harp snapped, their song stopped, and they cried in dismay—"Yes, that lost star was the best, she was the glory of all heavens!"

From that day the search is unceasing for her, and the cry goes on from one to the other that in her the world has lost its one joy!

Only in the deepest silence of night the stars smile and whisper among themselves—"Vain is this seeking! Unbroken perfection is over all!"

热词天地

1. splendour ['splendə(r)] *n.* 华丽；壮观
2. assembly [ə'semblɪ] *n.* 装配；集会

迷失的星星

当鸿蒙初辟,繁星第一次射出灿烂的光辉,众神在天上集会,唱着"呵,完美的画图,完全的快乐!"

有一位神忽然叫起来了——"光链里仿佛断了一环,一颗星星走失了。"

他们金琴的弦子猛然折断了,他们的歌声停止了,他们惊惶地叫着——"对了,那颗走失的星星是最美的,她是诸天的光荣!"

从那天起,他们不住地寻找她,众口相传地说,因为她丢失了,世界失去了一种快乐。

只在严静的夜里,众星微笑着互相低语说——"寻找是无用的,无缺的完美正笼盖着一切!"

Thou Keepest Me Free

By all means they try to hold me secure who love me in this world. But it is otherwise with thy love which is greater than theirs, and thou keepest me free.

Lest I forget them they never venture to leave me alone. But day passes by after day and thou art not seen.

If I call not thee in my prayers, if I keep not thee in my heart, thy love for me still waits for my love.

你让我自由

尘世上那些爱我的人，用尽方法拉住我。你的爱就不是那样，你的爱比他们的伟大得多，你让我自由。

他们从不敢离开我，恐怕我把他们忘掉。但是你，日子一天一天地过去，你还没有露面。

若是我不在祈祷中呼唤你，若是我不把你放在心上，你爱我的爱情仍在等待着我的爱。

Journey Home

The time that my journey takes is long and the way of it long.

I came out on the chariot of the first gleam[1] of light, and pursued my voyage through the wildernesses of worlds leaving my track on many a star and planet.

It is the most distant course that comes nearest to thyself, and that training is the most intricate[2] which leads to the utter simplicity of a tune.

The traveller has to knock at every alien door to come to his own, and one has to wander through all the outer worlds to reach the innermost shrine at the end.

My eyes strayed[3] far and wide before I shut them and said, "Here art thou!"

The question and the cry "Oh, where?" melt into tears of a thousand streams and deluge[4] the world with the flood of the assurance "I am!"

热词天地

1.gleam [gli:m] *vt.* & *vi.* （使）闪烁；（使）闪亮
2.intricate ['ɪntrɪkət] *adj.* 错综复杂的；难理解的
3.stray [streɪ] *vi.* 走失；偏离正题；走入歧途
4.deluge ['delju:dʒ] *n.* 洪水；泛滥；倾盆大雨

倦旅的家

我旅行的时间很长,旅途也是很长的。

天刚破晓,我就驱车起行,穿遍广漠的世界,在许多星球之上留下辙痕。

离你最近的地方,路途最远,最简单的音调,需要最艰苦的练习。

旅客要在每一个生人门口敲叩,才能敲到自己的家门,人要在外面到处漂流,最后才能走到最深的内殿。

我的眼睛向空阔处四望,最后才合上眼说:"你原来在这里!"

这句问话和呼唤"呵!在哪儿呢?",融化在千股的泪泉中,

和你保证的回答"我在这里!"的洪流,一同泛滥了全世界。

I Live in the Hope of Meeting with Him

The song that I came to sing remains unsung to this day.

I have spent my days in stringing and in unstringing my instrument.

The time has not come true, the words have not been rightly set; only there is the agony of wishing in my heart.

The blossom has not opened; only the wind is sighing by.

I have not seen his face, nor have I listened to his voice; only I have heard his gentle footsteps from the road before my house.

The livelong day has passed in spreading his seat on the floor; but the lamp has not been lit and I cannot ask him into my house.

I live in the hope of meeting with him; but this meeting is not yet.

我生活在与他相会的希望中

我要唱的歌,直到今天还没有唱出。

每天我总在乐器上调理弦索。
时间还没有到来,歌词也未曾填好;只有愿望的痛苦在我心中。
花蕊还未开放;只有风从旁叹息走过。

我没有看见过他的脸,也没有听见过他的声音;我只听见他轻蹑的足音,从我房前路上走过。悠长的一天消磨在为他在地上铺设座位;但是灯火还未点上,我不能请他进来。

我生活在和他相会的希望中,但这相会的日子还没有来到。

My Desires Are Many

My desires are many and my cry is pitiful, but ever didst thou save me by hard refusals; and this strong mercy has been wrought into my life through and through.

Day by day thou art making me worthy of the simple, great gifts that thou gavest to me unasked—this sky and the light, this body and the life and the mind—saving me from perils of overmuch desire.

There are times when I languidly linger and times when I awaken and hurry in search of my goal; but cruelly thou hidest thyself from before me.

Day by day thou art making me worthy of thy full acceptance by refusing me ever and anon, saving me from perils of weak, uncertain desire.

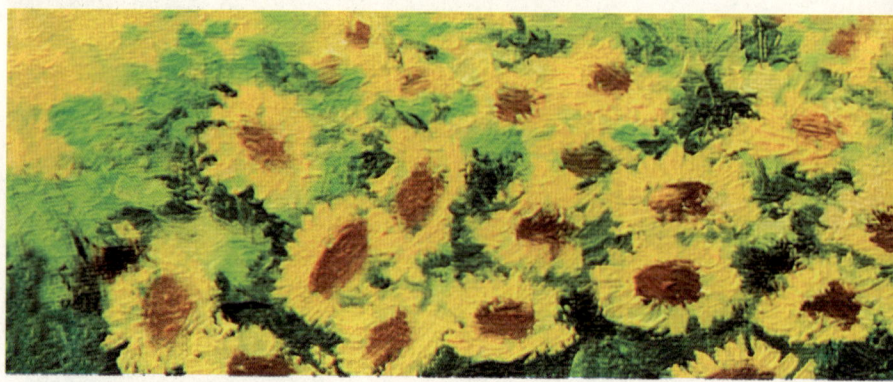

我的欲望很多

我的欲望很多，我的哭泣也很可怜，但你永远用坚决的拒绝来拯救我，这刚强的慈悲已经紧密地交织在我的生命里。

你使我一天一天的更配领受你自动的简单伟大的赐予——这天空和光明，这躯体和生命与心灵——把我从极欲的危险中拯救了出来。

有时候我懈怠地捱延，有时候我急忙警觉寻找我的路向；但是你却残忍地躲藏起来。

你不断地拒绝我，从软弱动摇的欲望的危险中拯救了我，使我一天一天的更配得你完全的接纳。

迷失的星星

Deity of the Ruined Temple

Deity of the ruined temple! The broken strings of Vina sing no more your praise. The bells in the evening proclaim not your time of worship. The air is still and silent about you.

In your desolate dwelling comes the vagrant spring breeze. It brings the tidings of flowers—the flowers that for your worship are offered no more.

Your worshipper of old wanders ever longing for favour still refused. In the eventide, when fires and shadows mingle with the gloom of dust, he wearily comes back to the ruined temple with hunger in his heart.

Many a festival day comes to you in silence, deity of the ruined temple.
Many a night of worship goes away with lamp unlit.

Many new images are built by masters of cunning art and carried to the holy stream of oblivion when their time is come.

Only the deity of the ruined temple remains unworshipped in deathless neglect.

破庙里的神呵

破庙里的神呵!七弦琴的断线不再弹唱赞美你的诗歌。晓钟也不再宣告礼拜你的时间。你周围的空气是寂静的。

流荡的春风来到你荒凉的居所。它带来了香花的消息——就是那素来供养你的香花,现在却无人来呈献了。

你的礼拜者,那些漂泊的惯旅,永远在企望那还未得到的恩典。黄昏来到,灯光明灭于尘影之中,他困乏地带着饥饿的心回到这破庙里来。

许多佳节都在静默中来到,破庙的神呵。
许多礼拜之夜,也在无火无灯中度过了。

精巧的艺术家,造了许多新的神像,当他们的末日来到了,便被抛入遗忘的圣河里。

只有破庙的神遗留在无人礼拜的、不死的冷淡之中。

I Love This Life

I was not aware of the moment when I first crossed the threshold of this life.

What was the power that made me open out into this vast mystery like a bud in the forest at midnight!

When in the morning I looked upon the light I felt in a moment that I was no stranger in this world, that the inscrutable without name and form had taken me in its arms in the form of my own mother.

Even so, in death the same unknown will appear as ever known to me. And because I love this life, I know I shall love death as well.

The child cries out when from the right breast the mother takes it away, in the very next moment to find in the left one its consolation.

我爱今生

当我刚跨过此生的门槛的时候,我并没有发觉。

是什么力量使我在这无边的神秘中开放,像一朵嫩蕊,中夜在森林里开花!

早起我看到光明,我立时觉得在这世界里我不是一个生人,那不可思议、不可名状的,已以我自己母亲的形象,把我抱在怀里。

就是这样,在死亡里,这同一的不可知者又要以我熟识的面目出现。因为我爱今生,我知道我也会一样地爱死亡。

当母亲从婴儿口中拿开右乳的时候,他就啼哭,但他立刻又从左乳得到了安慰。

I Will Deck Thee with Trophies

I will deck thee with trophies, garlands of my defeat. It is never in my power to escape unconquered.

I surely know my pride will go to the wall, my life will burst its bonds in exceeding pain, and my empty heart will sob out in music like a hollow reed, and the stone will melt in tears.

I surely know the hundred petals of a lotus will not remain closed for ever and the secret recess of its honey will be bared.

From the blue sky an eye shall gaze upon me and summon me in silence.

Nothing will be left for me, nothing whatever, and utter death shall I receive at thy feet.

我要以胜利品来装饰你

　　我要以胜利品,我的失败的花环,来装饰你。逃避不受征服,是我永远做不到的。

　　我准知道我的骄傲会碰壁,我的生命将因着极端的痛苦而炸裂,我的空虚的心将像一枝空苇呜咽出哀音,顽石也融成眼泪。

　　我准知道莲花的百瓣不会永远闭合,深藏的花蜜定将显露。
从碧空将有一只眼睛向我凝视,在默默地召唤我。
我将空无所有,绝对的空无所有,我将从你脚下领受绝对的死亡。

You and Me

That I should make much of myself and turn it on all sides, thus casting coloured shadows on thy radiance—such is thy maya.

Thou settest a barrier in thine own being and then callest thy severed self in myriad notes. This thy self-separation has taken body in me.

The poignant song is echoed through all the sky in many-coloured tears and smiles, alarms and hopes; waves rise up and sink again, dreams break and form. In me is thy own defeat of self.

This screen that thou hast raised is painted with innumerable figures with the brush of the night and the day. Behind it thy seat is woven in wondrous mysteries of curves, casting away all barren lines of straightness.

The great pageant of thee and me has overspread the sky. With the tune of thee and me all the air is vibrant, and all ages pass with the hiding and seeking of thee and me.

你和我

我应当自己发扬光大,四周放射,投映彩影于你的光辉之中——这便是你的幻境。

你在你自身里立起隔栏,用无数不同的音调来呼唤你的分身。
你这分身已在我体内成形。

高亢的歌声响彻诸天,在多彩的眼泪与微笑,震惊与希望中回应着;波起复落,梦破又圆。在我里面是你自身的破灭。

你卷起的那重帘幕,是用昼和夜的画笔,绘出了无数的花样。幕后的你的座位,是用奇妙神秘的曲线织成,抛弃了一切无聊的笔直的线条。

你我组成的伟丽的行列,布满了天空。因着你我的歌音,太空都在震颤,一切时代都在你我捉迷藏中度过了。

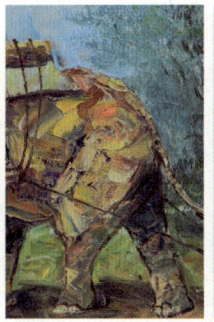

He It Is

He it is, the innermost one, who awakens my being with his deep hidden touches.

He it is who puts his enchantment upon these eyes and joyfully plays on the chords of my heart in varied cadence of pleasure and pain.

He it is who weaves the web of this maya in evanescent hues of gold and silver, blue and green, and lets peep out through the folds his feet, at whose touch I forget myself.

Days come and ages pass, and it is ever he who moves my heart in many a name, in many a guise, in many a rapture of joy and of sorrow.

就是他

就是他,那最深奥的,用他深隐的摩触使我清醒。

就是他把神符放在我的眼上,又快乐地在我心弦上弹弄出种种哀乐的调子。

就是他用金,银,青,绿的灵幻的色丝,织起幻境的披纱,他的脚趾从衣褶中外露。

在他的摩触之下,我忘却了自己。

日来年往,就是他永远以种种名字,种种姿态,种种的深悲和极乐,来打动我的心。

迷失的星星

Time Is Endless in Thy Hands

Time is endless in thy hands, my lord. There is none to count thy minutes.

Days and nights pass and ages bloom and fade like flowers. Thou knowest how to wait.

Thy centuries follow each other perfecting a small wild flower.

We have no time to lose, and having no time we must scramble for a chances. We are too poor to be late.

And thus it is that time goes by while I give it to every querulous man who claims it, and thine altar is empty of all offerings to the last.

At the end of the day I hasten in fear lest thy gate to be shut; but I find that yet there is time.

你手里的时光是无限的

你手里的光阴是无限的,我的主。你的分秒是无法计算的。
夜去明来,时代像花开花落。你晓得怎样来等待。

你的世纪,一个接着一个,来完成一朵小小的野花。
我们的光阴不能浪费,因为没有时间,我们必须争取机缘。我们太穷苦了,绝不可迟到。

因此,在我把时间让给每一个性急的,向我索要时间的人,我的时间就虚度了,最后你的神坛上就没有一点祭品。

一天过去,我赶忙前来,怕你的门已经关闭;但是我发现时间还有充裕。

Useless Lamp

On the slope of the desolate river among tall grasses I asked her, "Maiden, where do you go shading your lamp with your mantle? My house is all dark and lonesome—lend me your light!" she raised her dark eyes for a moment and looked at my face through the dusk. "I have come to the river," she said, "to float my lamp on the stream when the daylight wanes in the west." I stood alone among tall grasses and watched the timid flame of her lamp uselessly drifting in the tide.

In the silence of gathering night I asked her, "Maiden, your lights are all lit—then where do you go with your lamp? My house is all dark and lonesome—lend me your light." She raised her dark eyes on my face and stood for a moment doubtful. "I have come," she said at last, "to dedicate my lamp to the sky." I stood and watched her light uselessly burning in the void.

In the moonless gloom of midnight I ask her, "Maiden, what is your quest, holding the lamp near your heart? My house is all dark and lonesome—lend me your light." She stopped for a minute and thought and gazed at my face in the dark. "I have brought my light," she said, "to join the carnival of lamps." I stood and watched her little lamp uselessly lost among lights.

无用之灯

在荒凉的河岸上,深草丛中,我问她,"姑娘,你用披纱遮着灯,要到哪里去呢?我的房子黑暗寂寞——把你的灯借给我罢!"她抬起乌黑的眼睛,从暮色中看了我一会。"我到河边来,"她说,"要在太阳西下的时候,把我的灯飘浮到水上去。"我独立在深草中看着她的灯的微弱的火光,无用地在潮水上飘流。

在薄暮的寂静中,我问她,"你的灯火都已点上了——那么你拿着这灯到哪里去呢?我的房子黑暗寂寞——把你的灯借给我罢。"她抬起乌黑的眼睛望着我的脸,站着沉吟了一会。最后她说:"我来是要把我的灯献给上天。"我站着看她的灯光在天空中无用地燃点着。

在无月的夜半朦胧之中,我问她:"姑娘,你作什么把灯抱在心前呢?我的房子黑暗寂寞——把你的灯借给我罢。"她站住沉思了一会,在黑暗中注视着我的脸。她说:"我是带着我的灯,来参加灯节的。"我站着看着她的灯,无用地消失在众光之中。

Thou Givest Thyself to Me in Love

What divine drink wouldst thou have, my God, from this overflowing cup of my life?

My poet, is it thy delight to see thy creation through my eyes and to stand at the portals of my ears silently to listen to thine own eternal harmony?

Thy world is weaving words in my mind and thy joy is adding music to them. Thou givest thyself to me in love and then feelest thine own entire sweetness in me.

你把自己在梦中交给了我

我的上帝,从我满溢的生命之杯中,你要饮什么样的圣酒呢?

通过我的眼睛,来观看你自己的创造物,站在我的耳门上,来静听你自己的永恒的谐音,我的诗人,这是你的快乐吗?

你的世界在我的心灵里织上字句,你的快乐又给它们加上音乐。你把自己在梦中交给了我,又通过我来感觉你自己的完满的甜柔。

O Thou Beautiful

Thou art the sky and thou art the nest as well.

O thou beautiful, there in the nest is thy love that encloses the soul with colours and sounds and odours.

There comes the morning with the golden basket in her right hand bearing the wreath of beauty, silently to crown the earth.

And there comes the evening over the lonely meadows deserted by herds, through trackless paths, carrying cool draughts of peace in her golden pitcher from the western ocean of rest.

But there, where spreads the infinite sky for the soul to take her flight in, reigns the stainless white radiance. There is no day nor night, nor form nor colour, and never, never a word.

呵，美丽的你

你是天空，你也是窝巢。

呵，美丽的你，在窝巢里就是你的爱，用颜色，声音和香气来围拥住灵魂。

在那里，清晨来了，右手提着金筐，带着美的花环，静静地替大地加冕。

在那里，黄昏来了，越过无人畜牧的荒林，穿过车马绝迹的小径，在她的金瓶里带着安静的西方海上和平的凉飙。

但是在那里，纯白的光辉，统治着伸展着的为灵魂翱翔的无际的天空。在那里无昼无夜，无形无色，而且永远，永远无有言说。

The Arrival of the King

The night darkened. Our day's works had been done. We thought that the last guest had arrived for the night and the doors in the village were all shut. Only some said the king was to come. We laughed and said "No, it cannot be!"

It seemed there were knocks at the door and we said it was nothing but the wind. We put out the lamps and lay down to sleep. Only some said, "It is the messenger!" We laughed and said "No, it must be the wind!"

There came a sound in the dead of the night. We sleepily thought it was the distant thunder. The earth shook, the walls rocked, and it troubled us in our sleep. Only some said it was the sound of wheels. We said in a drowsy murmur, "No, it must be the rumbling of clouds!"

The night was still dark when the drum sounded. The voice came "Wake up! delay not!" We pressed our hands on our hearts and shuddered with fear. Some said, "Lo, there is the king's flag!" We stood up on our feet and cried "There is no time for delay!"

The king has come—but where are lights, where are wreaths? Where is the throne to seat him? Oh, shame! Oh utter shame! Where is the hall, the decorations? Someone has said, "Vain is this cry! Greet him with empty hands, lead him into thy rooms all bare!"

Open the doors, let the conch-shells be sounded! In the depth of the night has come the king of our dark, dreary house. The thunder roars in the sky. The darkness shudders with lightning. Bring out thy tattered piece of mat and spread it in the courtyard. With the storm has come of a sudden our king of the fearful night.

国王的到来

夜深了。我们一天的工作都已做完。我们以为投宿的客人都已来到，村里家家都已闭户了。只有几个人说，国王是要来的。我们笑了说："不会的，这是不可能的事！"

仿佛门上有敲叩的声音。我们说那不过是风。我们熄灯就寝。只有几个人说："这是使者！"我们笑了说："不是，这一定是风！"

在死沉沉的夜里传来一个声音。朦胧中我们以为是远远的雷响。墙摇地动，我们在睡眠里受了惊扰。只有几个人说："这是车轮的声音。"我们昏困地嘟哝着说："不是，这一定是雷响！"

鼓声响起的时候天还没亮。有声音喊着说："醒来罢！别耽误了！"我们拿手按住心口，吓得发抖。只有几个人说："看哪，这是国王的旗子！"我们爬起来站着叫："没有时间再耽误了！"

国王已经来了——但是灯火在哪里呢，花环在哪里呢？给他预备的宝座在哪里呢？呵，丢脸，呵，太丢脸了！客厅在哪里，陈设又在哪里呢？有几个人说了，"叫也无用了！用空手来迎接他罢，带他到你的空房里去罢！"

开起门来，吹起法螺罢！在深夜中国王降临到我黑暗凄凉的房子里了。空中雷声怒吼。黑暗和闪电一同颤抖。拿出你的破席铺在院子里罢。我们的国王在可怖之夜与暴风雨一同突然来到了。

迷失的星星

Thy Dreadful Sword

I thought I should ask of thee—but I dared not—the rose wreath thou hadst on thy neck. Thus I waited for the morning, when thou didst depart, to find a few fragments on the bed. And like a beggar I searched in the dawn only for a stray petal or two.

Ah me, what is it I find? What token left of thy love? It is no flower, no spices, no vase of perfumed water. It is thy mighty sword, flashing as a flame, heavy as a bolt of thunder. The young light of morning comes through the window and spread itself upon thy bed. The morning bird twitters and asks, "Woman, what hast thou got?" No, it is no flower, nor spices, nor vase of perfumed water—it is thy dreadful sword.

I sit and muse in wonder, what gift is this of thine. I can find no place to hide it. I am ashamed to wear it, frail as I am, and it hurts me when press it to my bosom. Yet shall I bear in my heart this honour of the burden of pain, this gift of thine.

From now there shall be no fear left for me in this world, and thou shalt be victorious in all my strife. Thou hast left death for my companion and I shall crown him with my life. Thy sword is with me to cut asunder my bonds, and there shall be no fear left for me in the world.

From now I leave off all petty decorations. Lord of my heart, no more shall there be for me waiting and weeping in corners, no more coyness and sweetness of demeanour. Thou hast given me thy sword for adornment. No more doll's decorations for me!

你的可畏的剑

我想我应当向你请求——可是我又不敢——你那挂在颈上的玫瑰花环。这样我等到早上,想在你离开的时候,从你床上找到些碎片。我像乞丐一样破晓就来寻找,只为着一两片散落的花瓣。

呵,我呵,我找到了什么呢?你留下了什么爱的标记呢?那不是花朵,不是香料,也不是一瓶香水。那是你的一把巨剑,火焰般放光,雷霆般沉重。清晨的微光从窗外射到床上。晨鸟喊喊喳喳着问:"女人,你得到了什么呢?"不,这不是花朵,不是香料,也不是一瓶香水——这是你的可畏的宝剑。

我坐着猜想,你这是什么礼物呢?我没有地方去藏放它。我不好意思佩带它;我是这样得柔弱,当我抱它在怀里的时候,它就把我压痛了。但是我要把这光宠铭记在心,你的礼物,这痛苦的负担。

从今起在这世界上我将没有畏惧,在我的一切奋斗中你将得到胜利。你留下死亡和我作伴,我将以我的生命给他加冕。我带着你的宝剑来斩断我的羁勒,在世界上我将没有畏惧。

从今起我要抛弃一切琐碎的装饰。我心灵的主,我不再在一隅等待哭泣,也不再畏怯娇羞。你已把你的宝剑给我佩带。我不再要玩偶的装饰品了!

Oh Awaken!

Languor is upon your heart and the slumber is still on your eyes. Has not the word come to you that the flower is reigning in splendour among thorns? Wake, oh awaken! let not the time pass in vain!

At the end of the stony path, in the country of virgin solitude, my friend is sitting all alone. Deceive him not. Wake, oh awaken!

What if the sky pants and trembles with the heat of the midday sun—what if the burning sand spreads its mantle of thirst—Is there no joy in the deep of your heart? At every footfall of yours, will not the harp of the road break out in sweet music of pain?

呵,醒来罢!

乏倦压在你的心上,你眼中尚有睡意。

你没有得到消息说荆棘丛中花朵正在盛开吗?醒来罢,呵,醒来!不要让光阴虚度了!

在石径的尽头,在幽静无人的田野里,我的朋友在独坐着。不要欺骗他罢。醒来,呵,醒来罢!

即使正午的骄阳使天空喘息摇颤——即使灼热的沙地展布开它干渴的巾衣——在你心的深处难道没有快乐吗?你的每一个足音,不会使道路的琴弦迸出痛苦的柔音吗?

I Stood Silent

I asked nothing from thee; I uttered not my name to thine ear. When thou took'st thy leave I stood silent. I was alone by the well where the shadow of the tree fell aslant, and the women had gone home with their brown earthen pitchers full to the brim. They called me and shouted, "Come with us, the morning is wearing on to noon." But I languidly lingered awhile lost in the midst of vague musings.

I heard not thy steps as thou camest. Thine eyes were sad when they fell on me; thy voice was tired as thou spokest low—"Ah, I am a thirsty traveller." I started up from my day-dreams and poured water from my jar on thy joined palms. The leaves rustled overhead; the cuckoo sang from the unseen dark, and perfume of babla flowers came from the bend of the road.

I stood speechless with shame when my name thou didst ask. Indeed, what had I done for thee to keep me in remembrance? But the memory that I could give water to thee to allay thy thirst will cling to my heart and enfold it in sweetness. The morning hour is late, the bird sings in weary notes, neem leaves rustle overhead and I sit and think and think.

我静静地站立

我不向你求什么；我不向你耳中陈述我的名字。当你离开的时候我静默地站着。我独立在树影横斜的井旁，女人们已顶着褐色的瓦罐盛满了水回家了。她们叫我说："和我们一块来罢，都快到了中午了。"但我仍在慵倦地留连，沉入恍惚的默想之中。

你走来时我没有听到你的足音。你含愁的眼望着我；你低语的时候声音是倦乏的——"呵，我是一个干渴的旅客。"我从幻梦中惊起把我罐里的水倒在你掬着的手掌里。树叶在头上萧萧地响着，杜鹃在幽暗处歌唱，曲径传来胶树的花香。

当你问到我的名字的时候，我羞得悄立无言。真的，我替你做了什么，值得你的忆念？但是我幸能给你饮水止渴的这段回忆，它将温馨地贴抱在我的心上。天已不早，鸟儿唱着倦歌，楝树叶子在头上沙沙作响，我坐着反复地想了又想。

Lies

When it was day they came into my house and said, "We shall only take the smallest room here."

They said, "We shall help you in the worship of your God and humbly accept only our own share in his grace"; and then they took their seat in a corner and they sat quiet and meek.

But in the darkness of night I find they break into my sacred shrine, strong and turbulent, and snatch with unholy greed the offerings from God's altar.

谎言

白天的时候,他们来到我的房子里说:"我们只占用最小的一间屋子。"

他们说:"我们要帮你礼拜你的上帝,而且只谦恭地领受我们应得的一份恩典";他们就在屋角安静谦柔地坐下。

但是在黑夜里,我发现他们强暴地冲进我的圣堂,贪婪地攫取了神坛上的祭品。

迷失的星星

The Gorgeous Constraint

The child who is decked with prince's robes and who has jewelled chains round his neck loses all pleasure in his play; his dress hampers him at every step.

In fear that it may be frayed, or stained with dust he keeps himself from the world, and is afraid even to move.

Mother, it is no gain, thy bondage of finery, if it keeps one shut off from the healthful dust of the earth, if it rob one of the right of entrance to the great fair of common human life.

华美的约束

那穿起王子的衣袍和挂起珠宝项链的孩子，在游戏中他失去了一切的快乐；他的衣服绊着他的步履。

为怕衣饰的破裂而污损，他不敢走进世界，甚至于不敢挪动。

母亲，这是毫无好处的，如你的华美的约束，使人和大地健康的尘土隔断，把人进入日常生活的盛大集会的权利剥夺去了。

Full of Sorrow

It is the pang of separation that spreads throughout the world and gives birth to shapes innumerable in the infinite sky.

It is this sorrow of separation that gazes in silence all nights from star to star and becomes lyric among rustling leaves in rainy darkness of July.

It is this overspreading pain that deepens into loves and desires, into sufferings and joy in human homes; and this it is that ever melts and flows in songs through my poet's heart.

离愁弥漫

离愁弥漫世界,在无际的天空中生出无数的情境。

就是这离愁整夜的悄望星辰,在七月阴雨之中,萧萧的树籁变成抒情的诗歌。

就是这笼压弥漫的痛苦,加深而成为爱、欲,而成为人间的苦乐;就是它永远通过诗人的心灵,融化流涌而成为诗歌。

第三卷 不再高声喧哗

飞鸟集

1

The world puts off its mask of vastness to its lover.
It becomes small as one song, as one kiss of the eternal[1].

热词天地

1. eternal [ɪ'tɜːnl] *adj.* 永恒的，永久的
   put off 脱去（衣、帽等）

面对它的爱人，世界摘下了它那广袤的面具。
它变小了，小如一首歌，小如一个永恒的吻。

2

If you shed[1] tears when you miss the sun,
you also miss the stars.

热词天地

1.shed [ʃed] *vt.* 流出；流下

如果你因错过太阳而流泪，
那么你也将错过群星了。

3

The sun goes to cross the Western sea,
leaving its last salutation[1] to the East.

热词天地

1.salutation [ˌsælju'teɪʃn] *n.* 招呼；致意

太阳横穿西海，向东方致以最后的敬礼。

4

In death the many becomes one;
in life the one becomes many.
Religion[1] will be one when God is dead.

热词天地

1.religion [rɪˈlɪdʒən] *n.* 宗教

死时，众多合而为一，
生时，一化为众多。
神死的时候，宗教将合而为一。

5

In darkness the One appears as uniform;
in the light the One appears as manifold[1].

热词天地

1. manifold ['mænɪfəʊld] *adj.* 多种多样的；多方面的

茫茫黑暗中，"一"仿若整体；
灼灼光亮中，"一"宛若众多。

6

The birth and death of the leaves are the rapid whirls[1] of the eddy[2]
whose wider circles move slowly among stars.

热词天地
1.whirl [wɜ:l] *vt.* 使旋转；使回旋
2.eddy ['edɪ] *n.* （水、烟等的）漩涡；涡流

绿叶的生与死是旋风的急骤旋转，
而更为广大的旋涡是在天上繁星间徐徐转动。

7

Death's stamp gives value to the coin of life; making it possible to buy with life what is truly precious[1].

热词天地

1.precious [preʃəs] *adj.* 宝贵的，珍贵的

死亡的印记给生的钱币以价值，使得真正的宝物可以用生命来购买。

8

The great is a born child; when he dies he gives his great childhood to the world.

伟人是一个天生的孩子，当他离世时，他把伟大的孩提时代给了世界。

9

The fountain of death makes the still[1] water of life play.

热词天地
1. still [stɪl] *adv.* 仍,仍然

平静的生命之水因死亡之泉而流动。

10

Darkness travels towards light, but blindness towards death.

黑暗向光明旅行,但盲目却奔向死亡。

11

Time is the wealth of change,
but the clock in its parody[1] makes it mere[2] change and no wealth.

热词天地

1. parody ['pærədɪ] *n.* 拙劣的模仿；恶搞
2. mere [mɪə(r)] *adj.* 仅仅；只不过

时光是变化的财富，
但时钟模仿它，却令时光只有变化，没有财富。

12

This life is the crossing of a sea,
where we meet in the same narrow ship.
In death we reach the shore and go to our different worlds.

生命就似穿越大海，
在那里我们相聚在狭窄的小船。
死亡时，我们便到了对岸，各奔天涯。

13

Death belongs to life as birth does.
The walk is in the raising of the foot as in the laying of it down.

热词天地

belong to 属于；是（某团体、国家等）的成员

死亡就像诞生一样，同属于生命。
举足是走路，正如落足也是走路。

14

I shall die again and again to know that life is inexhaustible[1].

热词天地

1.inexhaustible [ˌɪnɪgˈzɔːstəbl] *adj.* 无穷无尽的，用不完的
again and again 再三地，反复地

我将一次又一次地死去，来懂得生命的无休无止。

15

I have suffered[1] and despaired[2] and known death
and I am glad that I am in this great world.

热词天地

1.suffer [ˈsʌfə(r)] *vt.* 忍受；容忍
2.despair [dɪˈspeə(r)] *n.* 绝望；使人绝望的人（或事物）

我曾受过苦，曾失望过，也曾领教过死亡，
于是我以在这伟大的世界里为乐。

流萤集

1

The glow-worm while exploring the dust
never knows that stars are in the sky.

萤火虫在尘土中探索时，
从不知道天空中星星的存在。

2

Though the thorn in thy flower pricked me,
O Beauty,
I am grateful.

虽然你花间的荆棘刺痛了我
美人啊,
我仍然感激不尽。

3

The darkness of night, like pain, is dumb,
the darkness of dawn, like peace, is silent.

夜晚的黑暗,喑哑无声,如若痛苦,
黎明的黑暗,静默不语,如同和平。

4

Bigotry tries to keep truth safe in its hand
with a grip that kills it.
Wishing to hearten a timid lamp
great night lights all her stars.

偏执想将真理安全地握在手里,
真理却死在它紧握的手心。
愿望想燃起一盏羞怯的灯火,
广阔的夜空点亮了满天繁星。

5

The world knows that the few
are more than the many.

举世皆知,
少数胜于众多。

6

Pride engraves his frowns in stone,
love offers her surrender in flowers.

骄傲将紧蹙的眉头刻进顽石,
爱情对她的降臣奉上鲜花。

7

In its swelling pride
the bubble doubts the truth of the sea,
and laughs and bursts into emptiness.

泡泡因骄傲而膨胀,
质疑大海的真实,
因讥笑而爆裂成空无一物。

8

Love is an endless mystery,
for it has nothing else to explain it.

爱情是一道永无止境的谜题,
因为它除此之外无从解释。

9

You leave your memory as a flame
to my lonely lamp of separation.

你留下火焰般的回忆
在我别离的孤灯里。

10

I came to offer thee a flower,
but thou must have all my garden,
it is thine.

我来向你献上一枝花,
可你一定要把我整座花园都揽下,
好吧,全是你的。

园丁集 （冰心译）

1

None lives forever, brother, and nothing lasts for long. Keep that in mind and rejoice[1].

Our life is not the one old burden, our path is not the one long journey.

One sole[2] poet has not to sing one aged song.

The flower fades and dies; but he who wears the flower has not to mourn[3] for it forever.

Brother, keep that in mind and rejoice.

There must come a full pause to weave perfection into music.

Life droops toward its sunset to be drowned in the golden shadows.

Love must be called from its play to drink sorrow and be borne to the heaven of tears.

Brother, keep that in mind and rejoice.

We hasten to gather our flowers lest[4] they are plundered[5] by the passing winds.

It quickens our blood and brightens our eyes to snatch[6] kisses that would vanish if we delayed.

Our life is eager, our desires are keen, for time tolls the bell of parting.

Brother, keep that in mind and rejoice.

There is not time for us to clasp[7] a thing and crush[8] it and fling it away to the dust.

The hours trip rapidly away, hiding their dreams in their skirts.

Our life is short; it yields but a few days for love.

Were it for work and drudgery it would be endlessly long.

Brother, keep that in mind and rejoice.

Beauty is sweet to us, because she dances to the same fleeting tune with our lives.

Knowledge is precious to us, because we shall never have time to complete it.

All is done and finished in the eternal Heaven.

But earth's flowers of illusion are kept eternally fresh by death.

Brother, keep that in mind and rejoice.

热词天地

1. rejoice [rɪ'dʒɔɪs] *vt.* 使高兴；使欢喜
2. sole [səʊl] *adj.* 单独的；惟一的
3. mourn [mɔːn] *vt.* 表示深深的遗憾；哀悼
4. lest [lest] *conj.* 唯恐；以免
5. plunder ['plʌndə(r)] *vt.* & *vi.* 掠夺；偷
6. snatch [snætʃ] *vt.* 抢夺；夺得
7. clasp [klɑːsp] *n.* 扣钩，扣环
8. crush [krʌʃ] *vt.* 压破，压碎　*vi.* 挤

没有人永远活着,弟兄,没有东西能以经久。把这紧记在心及时行乐吧。
我们的生命不是那个旧的负担,我们的道路不是那条长的旅程。
一个单独的诗人,不必去唱一支旧歌。
花儿萎谢;但是戴花的人不必永远悲伤。
弟兄,把这个紧记在心及时行乐吧。

必须有一段完全的停歇,好把"圆满"编进音乐。
生命向它的黄昏下落,为了沉浸于金影之中。
必须从游戏中把"爱"招回,去饮忧伤之酒,再去生于泪天。
弟兄,把这紧记在心及时行乐吧。

我们忙去采花,怕被过路的风偷走。
去夺取稍纵即逝的接吻,使我们血液奔流双目发光。
我们的生命是热切的,愿望是强烈的,因为时间在敲着离别之钟。
弟兄,把这紧记在心及时行乐吧。

我们没有时间去把握一件事物,揉碎它又把它丢在地上。
时间急速地走过,把梦幻藏在裙底。
我们的生命是短促的,只有几天恋爱的工夫。
若是为工作和劳役,生命就变得无尽的漫长。
弟兄,把这紧记在心及时行乐吧。

美对我们是甜柔的,因为她和我们生命的快速调子应节舞蹈。
知识对我们是宝贵的,因为我们永不会有时间去完成它。
一切都在永生的天上做完。但是大地的幻象的花朵,却被死亡保持得永远新鲜。
弟兄,把这紧记在心及时行乐吧。

2

The day is not yet done, the fair is not over, the fair on the river bank.

I had feared that my time had been squandered[1] and my last penny lost.

But no, my brother, I have still something left. My fate has not cheated me of everything.

The selling and buying are over.

All the dues on both sides have been gathered in, and it is time for me to go home.

But, gatekeeper, do you ask for your toll[2]?

Do not fear, I have still something left. My fate has not cheated me of everything.

The lull[3] in the wind threatens storm, and the lowering clouds in the west bode no good.

The hushed water waits for the wind.

I hurry to cross the river before the night overtakes[4] me.

O ferryman, you want your fee!

Yes, brother, I have still something left. My fate has not cheated me of everything.

In the wayside under the tree sits the beggar. Alas[5], he looks at my face with a timid hope!

He thinks I am rich with the day's profit.

Yes, brother, I have still something left. My fate has not cheated me of everything.

The night grows dark and the road lonely. Fireflie[6]'s gleam among the leaves.

Who are you that follow me with stealthy[7] silent steps?

Ah, I know, it is your desire to rob me of all my gains. I will not disappoint you!

For I still have something left, and my fate has not cheated me of everything.

At midnight I reach home. My hands are empty.

You are waiting with anxious eyes at my door, sleepless and silent.

Like a timorous[8] bird you fly to my breast with eager love.

Ay, ay, my God, much remains still. My fate has not cheated me of everything.

热词天地

1. squander ['skwɒndə(r)] *v.* 挥霍，浪费
2. toll [təʊl] *vt.* 向……征收捐税；向……收通行费
3. lull [lʌl] *n.* 暂停；间歇
4. overtake [ˌəʊvə'teɪk] *vt.* 追上，赶上
5. alas [ə'læs] *int.* （表示悲痛、遗憾）哎呀
6. firefly ['faɪəflaɪ] *n.* 萤火虫
7. stealthy ['stelθɪ] *adj.* 悄悄的；鬼鬼祟祟的
8. timorous ['tɪmərəs] *adj.* 胆怯的；羞怯的

白日未尽，河岸上的市集未散。
我只恐我的时间浪掷了，我的最后一文钱也丢掉了。
但是，没有，我的兄弟，我还有些剩余，命运并没有把我的一切都骗走。

买卖做完了。
两边的手续费都收过了，该是我回家的时候了。
但是，看门的，你要你的辛苦钱吗？
别怕，我还有点剩余，命运并没有把我的一切都骗走。

风声宣布着风暴的威胁，西方低垂的云影预报着恶兆。
静默的河水在等候着狂风。
我怕被黑夜赶上，急忙过河。
啊，船夫，你要收费！
是的，兄弟，我还有些剩余，命运并没有把我的一切都骗走。

路边树下坐着一个乞丐，可怜啊，他含着羞怯的希望看着我的脸！
他以为我富足地携带着一天的利润。
是的，兄弟，我还有点剩余，命运并没有把我的一切都骗走。

夜色愈深，路上静寂，萤火虫在草间闪烁。
谁以悄悄的蹑步在跟着我？
啊，我知道了，你想掠夺我的一切获得。我必不使你失望！
因为我还有些剩余，命运并没有把我的一切都骗走。

夜半到家。我两手空空。
你带着切望的眼睛，在门前等我，无眠而静默。
像一只羞怯的鸟，你满怀爱热地飞到我胸前。
唉，唉，我的神，我还有许多剩余。命运并没有把我的一切都骗走。

吉檀迦利 （冰心 译）

No More Noisy Loud Words

No more noisy, loud words from me—such is my master's will. Henceforth I deal in whispers. The speech of my heart will be carried on in murmurings of a song.

Men hasten to the King's market. All the buyers and sellers are there. But I have my untimely leave in the middle of the day, in the thick of work.

Let then the flowers come out in my garden, though it is not their time; and let the midday bees strike up their lazy hum.

Full many an hour have I spent in the strife of the good and the evil, but now it is the pleasure of my playmate of the empty days to draw my heart on to him; and I know not why is this sudden call to what useless inconsequence!

不再高声喧哗

我不再高谈阔论了——这是我主的意旨。从那时起我轻声细语。我心里的话要用歌曲低唱出来。

人们急急忙忙地到国王的市场上去,买卖的人都在那里,但在工作正忙的正午,我就早早地离开。

那就让花朵在我的园中开放,虽然花时未到;让蜜蜂在中午奏起慵懒的嗡哼。

我曾把充分的时间,用在理欲交战里,但如今是我暇日游侣的雅兴,把我的心拉到他那里去;我也不知道这忽然的召唤,会引到什么突出的奇景!

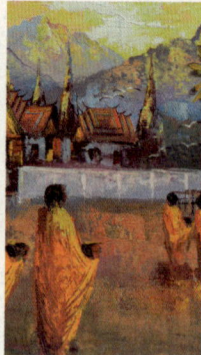
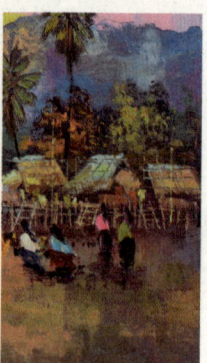

Closed Path

I thought that my voyage[1] had come to its end at the last limit of my power,—that the path before me was closed, that provisions were exhausted and the time come to take shelter in a silent obscurity.

But I find that thy will knows no end in me. And when old words die out on the tongue, new melodies break forth from the heart; and where the old tracks are lost, new country is revealed with its wonders.

热词天地

1. voyage ['vɔɪdʒ] *n.* 旅行，航海，航空
   come to end 进入尾声
   die out （指物种、家族、习惯、观念等）绝迹，消失；绝种

山穷水尽

我以为我的精力已竭,旅程已终——前路已绝,储粮已尽,退隐在静默鸿蒙中的时间已经到来。

但是我发现你的意志在我身上不知有终点。旧的言语刚在舌尖上死去,新的音乐又从心上进来;旧辙方迷,新的田野又在面前奇妙地展开。

Lost Time

On many an idle day have I grieved over lost time. But it is never lost, my lord. Thou hast taken every moment of my life in thine own hands.

Hidden in the heart of things thou art nourishing[1] seeds into sprouts[2], buds into blossoms, and ripening flowers into fruitfulness.

I was tired and sleeping on my idle bed and imagined all work had ceased. In the morning I woke up and found my garden full with wonders of flowers.

热词天地

1. nourish ['nʌrɪʃ] *vt.* 滋养；施肥于
2. sprout [spraʊt] *vt.* 使发芽；使生长
   many a 许多
   grieve over 对……感到伤心；悼念

蹉跎岁月

在许多闲散的日子,我悼惜着虚度了的光阴。但是光阴并没有虚度,我的主。你掌握了我生命里寸寸的光阴。

你潜藏在万物的心里,培育着种子发芽,蓓蕾绽红,花落结实。

我困乏了,在闲榻上睡眠,想象一切工作都已停歇。早晨醒来,我发现我的园里,却开遍了异蕊奇花。

Let Me Not Forget a Moment

If it is not my portion to meet thee in this life then let me ever feel that I have missed thy sight—let me not forget for a moment, let me carry the pangs of this sorrow in my dreams and in my wakeful hours.

As my days pass in the crowded market of this world and my hands grow full with the daily profits, let me ever feel that I have gained nothing—let me not forget for a moment, let me carry the pangs of this sorrow in my dreams and in my wakeful hours.

When I sit by the roadside, tired and panting, when I spread my bed low in the dust, let me ever feel that the long journey is still before me—let me not forget a moment, let me carry the pangs of this sorrow in my dreams and in my wakeful hours.

When my rooms have been decked out and the flutes sound and the laughter there is loud, let me ever feel that I have not invited thee to my house—let me not forget for a moment, let me carry the pangs of this sorrow in my dreams and in my wakeful hours.

让我念念不忘

假如我今生无份遇到你,就让我永远感到恨不相逢——让我念念不忘,让我在醒时梦中都怀带着这悲哀的苦痛。

当我的日子在世界的闹市中度过,我的双手满捧着每日的赢利的时候,让我永远觉得我是一无所获——让我念念不忘,让我在醒时梦中都带着这悲哀的苦痛。

当我坐在路边,疲乏喘息,当我在尘土中铺设卧具,让我永远记着前面还有悠悠的长路——让我念念不忘,让我在醒时梦中都怀带着悲哀的苦痛。

当我的屋子装饰好了,箫笛吹起,欢笑声喧的时候,让我永远觉得我还没有请你光临——让我念念不忘,让我在醒时梦中都怀带着这悲哀的苦痛。

In One Salutation to Thee

In one salutation to thee, my God, let all my senses spread out and touch this world at thy feet.

Like a rain-cloud of July hung low with its burden of unshed showers let all my mind bend down at thy door in one salutation to thee.

Let all my songs gather together their diverse strains into a single current and flow to a sea of silence in one salutation to thee.

Like a flock of homesick cranes flying night and day back to their mountain nests let all my life take its voyage to its eternal home in one salutation to thee.

在我向你合十膜拜

在我向你合十膜拜之中,我的上帝,让我一切的感知都舒展在你的脚下,接触这个世界。

像七月的湿云,带着未落的雨点沉沉下垂,在我向你合十膜拜之中,让我的全副心灵在你的门前俯伏。

让我所有的诗歌,聚集起不同的调子,在我向你合十膜拜之中,成为一股洪流,倾注入静寂的大海。

像一群思乡的鹤鸟,日夜飞向他们的山巢,在我向你合十膜拜之中,让我全部的生命,启程回到它永久的家乡。

And You Sit There Smiling

I boasted among men that I had known you. They see your pictures in all works of mine. They come and ask me, "Who is he?" I know not how to answer them. I say, "Indeed, I cannot tell." They blame me and they go away in scorn. And you sit there smiling.

I put my tales of you into lasting songs. The secret gushes out from my heart. They come and ask me, "Tell me all your meanings." I know not how to answer them. I say, "Ah, who knows what they mean!" They smile and go away in utter scorn. And you sit there smiling.

你却坐在那里微笑

　　我在人前夸说我认得你。在我的作品中,他们看到了你的画像,他们走来问:"他是谁?"我不知道怎么回答。我说,"真的,我说不出来。"他们斥责我,轻蔑地走开了。你却坐在那里微笑。

　　我把你的事迹编成不朽的诗歌。秘密从我心中涌出。他们走来问我:"把所有的意思都告诉我们罢。"我不知道怎样回答。我说:"呵,谁知道那是什么意思!"他们哂笑了,鄙夷之极地走开。你却坐在那里微笑。

I Sought Thee with My Songs

Ever in my life have I sought thee with my songs. It was they who led me from door to door, and with them have I felt about me, searching and touching my world.

It was my songs that taught me all the lessons I ever learnt; they showed me secret paths, they brought before my sight many a star on the horizon of my heart.

They guided me all the day long to the mysteries of the country of pleasure and pain, and, at last, to what palace gate have they brought me in the evening at the end of my journey?

我以诗歌来寻求你

我这一生永远以诗歌来寻求你。它们领我从这门走到那门,我和它们一同摸索,寻求着,接触着我的世界。

我所学过的功课,都是诗歌教给我的;它们把捷径指示给我,它们把我心里地平线上的许多星辰,带到我的眼前。

它们整天地带领我走向苦痛和快乐的神秘之国,最后,在我旅程终点的黄昏,它们要把我带到哪一座宫殿的门首呢?

Waiting for Him in Vain

The night is nearly spent waiting for him in vain. I fear lest in the morning he suddenly come to my door when I have fallen asleep wearied out. Oh friends, leave the way open to him—forbid him not.

If the sounds of his steps does not wake me, do not try to rouse me, I pray. I wish not to be called from my sleep by the clamorous choir of birds, by the riot of wind at the festival of morning light. Let me sleep undisturbed even if my lord comes of a sudden to my door.

Ah, my sleep, precious sleep, which only waits for his touch to vanish. Ah, my closed eyes that would open their lids only to the light of his smile when he stands before me like a dream emerging from darkness of sleep.

Let him appear before my sight as the first of all lights and all forms. The first thrill of joy to my awakened soul let it come from his glance. And let my return to myself be immediate return to him.

等他又落了空

夜已将尽,等他又落了空。我怕在清晨我正倦睡的时候,他忽然来到我的门前。呵,朋友们,给他开着门罢——不要拦阻他。

若是他的脚步声没有把我惊醒,请不要叫醒我。我不愿意小鸟嘈杂的合唱,和庆祝晨光的狂欢的风声,把我从睡梦中吵醒。即使我的主突然来到我的门前,也让我无扰地睡着。

呵,我的睡眠,宝贵的睡眠,只等着他的摩触来消散。呵,我的合着的眼,只在他微笑的光中才开睫,当他像从洞黑的睡眠里浮现的梦一般地站立在我面前。

让他作为最初的光明和形象,来呈现在我的眼前。让他的眼光成为我觉醒的灵魂最初的欢跃。让我自我的返回成为向他立地的皈依。

My King

The day was when I did not keep myself in readiness for thee; and entering my heart unbidden even as one of the common crowd, unknown to me, my king, thou didst press the signet of eternity upon many a fleeting moment of my life.

And today when by chance I light upon them and see thy signature, I find they have lain scattered in the dust mixed with the memory of joys and sorrows of my trivial days forgotten.

Thou didst not turn in contempt from my childish play among dust, and the steps that I heard in my playroom are the same that are echoing from star to star.

我的国王

那天我没有准备好来等候你,我的国王,你就像一个素不相识的平凡的人,自动地进到我的心里,在我生命的许多流逝的时光中,盖上了永生的印记。

今天我偶然照见了你的签印,我发现它们和我遗忘了的日常哀乐的回忆,杂乱地散掷在尘埃里。

你不曾鄙夷地避开我童年时代在尘土中的游戏,我在游戏室里所听见的足音,和在群星中的回响是相同的。

I Am Eager to Die into the Deathless

I dive down into the depth of the ocean of forms, hoping to gain the perfect pearl of the formless.

No more sailing from harbour to harbour with this my weather-beaten boat. The days are long passed when my sport was to be tossed on waves.

And now I am eager to die into the deathless.

Into the audience hall by the fathomless abyss where swells up the music of toneless strings I shall take this harp of my life.

I shall tune it to the notes of forever, and when it has sobbed out its last utterance, lay down my silent harp at the feet of the silent.

我渴望死于不死之中

我跳进形象海洋的深处,希望能得到那无形象的完美的珍珠。

我不再以我的旧船去走遍海港,我乐于弄潮的日子早已过去了。

现在我渴望死于不死之中。

我要拿起我的生命的弦琴,进入无底深渊旁边,那座涌出无调的乐音的广厅。

我要调拨我的琴弦,和永恒的乐音合拍,当它呜咽出最后的声音时,就把我静默的琴儿放在静默的脚边。

At This Time of My Parting

At this time of my parting, wish me good luck, my friends! The sky is flushed with the dawn and my path lies beautiful.

Ask not what I have with me to take there. I start on my journey with empty hands and expectant heart.

I shall put on my wedding garland. Mine is not the red-brown dress of the traveller, and though there are dangers on the way I have no fear in mind.

The evening star will come out when my voyage is done and the plaintive notes of the twilight melodies be struck up from the King's gateway.

在我动身的时光

在我动身的时光,祝我一路福星罢,我的朋友们!天空里晨光辉煌,我的前途是美丽的。

不要问我带些什么到那边去。我只带着空空的手和企望的心。

我要戴上我婚礼的花冠。我穿的不是红褐色的行装,虽然间关险阻,我心里也没有惧怕。

旅途尽处,晚星将生,从王宫的门口将弹出黄昏的凄乐。

Come Silently and Take Thy Seat Here

When I give up the helm I know that the time has come for thee to take it. What there is to do will be instantly done. Vain is this struggle.

Then take away your hands and silently put up with your defeat, my heart, and think it your good fortune to sit perfectly still where you are placed.

These my lamps are blown out at every little puff of wind, and trying to light them I forget all else again and again.

But I shall be wise this time and wait in the dark, spreading my mat on the floor; and whenever it is thy pleasure, my lord, come silently and take thy seat here.

悄悄地走来坐下罢

当我放下舵盘，我知道你来接收的时候到了。当做的事立刻要做了。挣扎是无用的。

那就把手拿开，静默地承认失败罢，我的心呵，要想到能在你的岗位上默坐，还算是幸运的。

我的几盏灯都被一阵阵的微风吹灭了，为想把它们重新点起，我屡屡地把其他的事情都忘却了。

这次我要聪明一点，把我的席子铺在地上，在暗中等候；什么时候你高兴，我的主，悄悄地走来坐下罢。

I Find Her Not

In desperate hope I go and search for her in all the corners of my room; I find her not.

My house is small and what once has gone from it can never be regained.
But infinite is thy mansion, my lord, and seeking her I have to come to thy door.

I stand under the golden canopy of thine evening sky and I lift my eager eyes to thy face.
I have come to the brink of eternity from which nothing can vanish—no hope, no happiness, no vision of a face seen through tears.

Oh, dip my emptied life into that ocean, plunge it into the deepest fullness. Let me for once feel that lost sweet touch in the allness of the universe.

我找不到她

在无望的希望中,我在房里的每一个角落找她;我找不到她。

我的房子很小,一旦丢了东西就永远找不回来。
但是你的房子是无边无际的,我的主,为着找她,我来到了你的门前。

我站在你薄暮金色的天穹下,向你抬起渴望的眼。
我来到了永恒的边涯,在这里万物不灭——无论是希望,是幸福,或是从泪眼中望见的人面。

呵,把我空虚的生命浸到这海洋里罢,跳进这最深的完满里罢。让我在宇宙的完整里,感觉一次那失去的温馨的接触罢。

Whisper to Me!

O thou the last fulfilment of life, Death, my death, come and whisper to me!

Day after day I have kept watch for thee; for thee have I borne the joys and pangs of life.

All that I am, that I have, that I hope and all my love have ever flowed towards thee in depth of secrecy. One final glance from thine eyes and my life will be ever thine own.

The flowers have been woven and the garland is ready for the bridegroom. After the wedding the bride shall leave her home and meet her lord alone in the solitude of night.

对我低语罢!

呵,你这生命最后的完成,死亡,我的死亡,来对我低语罢!

我天天地在守望着你;为你,我忍受着生命中的苦乐。

我的一切存在,一切所有,一切希望,和一切的爱,总在深深的秘密中向你奔流。你的眼泪向我最后一盼,我的生命就永远是你的。

花环已为新郎编好。婚礼行过,新娘就要离家,在静夜里和她的主人独对了。

I Must Launch Out My Boat

I must launch out my boat. The languid hours pass by on the shore—Alas for me!

The spring has done its flowering and taken leave. And now with the burden of faded futile flowers I wait and linger.

The waves have become clamorous, and upon the bank in the shady lane the yellow leaves flutter and fall.

What emptiness do you gaze upon! Do you not feel a thrill passing through the air with the notes of the far-away song floating from the other shore?

我必须撑出我的船去

我必须撑出我的船去。时光都在岸边捱延消磨了——不堪的我呵！

春天把花开过就告别了。如今落红遍地，我却等待而又留连。
潮声渐喧，河岸的荫滩上黄叶飘落。

你凝望着的是何等的空虚！你不觉得有一阵惊喜和对岸遥远的歌声从天空中一同飘来吗？

Do Not Pass by Like a Dream

In the deep shadows of the rainy July, with secret steps, thou walkest, silent as night, eluding all watchers.

Today the morning has closed its eyes, heedless of the insistent calls of the loud east wind, and a thick veil has been drawn over the ever-wakeful blue sky.

The woodlands have hushed their songs, and doors are all shut at every house. Thou art the solitary wayfarer in this deserted street. Oh my only friend, my best beloved, the gates are open in my house—do not pass by like a dream.

不要像梦一般地走过

在七月霪雨的浓阴中,你用秘密的脚步行走,夜一般的轻悄,躲过一切守望的人。

今天,清晨闭上眼,不理连连呼喊的狂啸的东风,一张厚厚的纱幕遮住永远清醒的碧空。

林野住了歌声,家家闭户。在这冷寂的街上,你是孤独的行人。呵,我唯一的朋友,我最爱的人,我的家门是开着的——不要梦一般的走过罢。

We Sail in a Boat Together

Early in the day it was whispered that we should sail in a boat, only thou and I, and never a soul in the world would know of this our pilgrimage to no country and to no end.

In that shoreless ocean, at thy silently listening smile my songs would swell in melodies, free as waves, free from all bondage of words.

Is the time not come yet? Are there works still to do? Lo, the evening has come down upon the shore and in the fading light the seabirds come flying to their nests.

Who knows when the chains will be off, and the boat, like the last glimmer of sunset, vanish into the night?

我们一同去泛舟

在清晓的密语中,我们约定了同去泛舟,世界上没有一个人知道我们这无目的无终止的遨游。

在无边的海洋上,在你静听的微笑中,我的歌唱抑扬成调,像海波一般的自由,不受字句的束缚。

时间还没有到吗?你还有工作要做吗?看罢,暮色已经笼罩海岸,苍茫里海鸟已群飞归巢。

谁知道什么时候可以解开链索,这只船会像落日的余光,消融在黑夜之中呢?

When One Knows Thee

Thou hast made me known to friends whom I knew not. Thou hast given me seats in homes not my own. Thou hast brought the distant near and made a brother of the stranger.

I am uneasy at heart when I have to leave my accustomed shelter; I forget that there abides the old in the new, and that there also thou abidest.

Through birth and death, in this world or in others, wherever thou leadest me it is thou, the same, the one companion of my endless life who ever linkest my heart with bonds of joy to the unfamiliar.

When one knows thee, then alien there is none, then no door is shut. Oh, grant me my prayer that I may never lose the bliss of the touch of the one in the play of many.

当有人认识了你

你使不相识的朋友认识了我。你在别人家里给我准备了座位。你缩短了距离,你把生人变成弟兄。

在我必须离开故居的时候,我心里不安;我忘了是旧人迁入新居,而且你也住在那里。

通过生和死,今生或来世,无论你带领我到哪里,都是你,仍是你,我的无穷生命中的唯一伴侣,永远用欢乐的系缧,把我的心和陌生的人联系在一起。

当有人认识了你,世上就没有陌生的人,也没有了紧闭的门户。呵,请允许我的祈求,使我在与众生游戏之中,永不失去和你单独接触的福祉。

Is It Beyond Thee to Be Glad with This Rhythm?

Is it beyond thee to be glad with the gladness of this rhythm? To be tossed and lost and broken in the whirl of this fearful joy?

All things rush on, they stop not, they look not behind, no power can hold them back, they rush on.

Keeping steps with that restless, rapid music, seasons come dancing and pass away—colours, tunes, and perfumes pour in endless cascades in the abounding joy that scatters and gives up and dies every moment.

这音律不能使你高兴吗?

这欢欣的音律不能使你欢欣吗？不能使你回旋激荡，消失碎裂在这可怖的快乐旋转之中吗？

万物急遽地前奔，它们不停留也不回顾，任何力量都不能挽住它们，它们急遽地前奔。

季候应和着这急速不宁的音乐，跳舞着来了又去——颜色，声音，香味在这充溢的快乐里，汇注成奔流无尽的瀑泉，时时刻刻地在散溅,退落而死亡。

I Have No Sleep Tonight

Art thou abroad on this stormy night on thy journey of love, my friend? The sky groans like one in despair.

I have no sleep tonight. Ever and again I open my door and look out on the darkness, my friend!

I can see nothing before me. I wonder where lies thy path!

By what dim shore of the ink-black river, by what far edge of the frowning forest, through what mazy depth of gloom art thou threading thy course to come to me, my friend?

我今夜无眠

在这暴风雨的夜晚你还在外面作爱的旅行吗,我的朋友?天空像失望者在哀号。

我今夜无眠,我不断地开门向黑暗中瞭望,我的朋友!

我什么都看不见。我不知道你要走哪一条路!

是从墨黑的河岸上,是从远远的愁惨的树林边,是穿过昏暗迂回的曲径,你摸索着来到我这里吗,我的朋友?

第四卷
面对面

飞鸟集

1

Do not linger[1] to gather flowers to keep them, but walk on, for flowers will keep themselves blooming all your way.

热词天地

1.linger ['lɪŋgə(r)] vi. 逗留，徘徊

只管走过去，不要逗留着采集花朵，
你的路上自有鲜花绽放。

2

That I exist is a perpetual[1] surprise which is life.

热词天地

1.perpetual [pə'petʃuəl] *adj.* 永久的；不断的

我的存在是一个永恒的奇迹，
这就是生活。

3

I cannot choose the best.
The best chooses me.

我无法选择最好，
最好选择了我。

4

Man is a born child, his power is the power of growth.

人是一个初生的孩子,
他的力量就是成长的力量。

5

He who wants to do good knocks at the gate;
he who loves finds the gate open.

想要做好事的人,在外面敲着门;
仁爱之人看见门是敞开的。

6

The flaming fire warns me off by its own glow.
Save me from the dying embers[1] hidden under ashes.

热词天地

1. ember ['embə(r)] *n.* 余烬；余火
   warn off 不许……上前
   save from 从……中救出，使免受

燃烧的火，以它的熊熊火焰警告我不要走近。
把我从隐藏在灰土中的余烬里救出来吧。

7

Who drives me forward like fate?
The myself striding[1] on my back.

热词天地

1.stride [straɪd] *vt.* & *vi.* 大踏步走；跨过

谁像命运般地催促我前行？
惟有在身后大步行走的我自己。

8

Those who have everything but thee, my God,
laugh at those who have nothing but thyself.

热词天地

laugh at 因……而发笑；嘲笑；蔑视

那些拥有一切却独缺了您的人，我的上帝，
在讥笑那些双手空空而只有您的人呢。

9

God's right hand is gentle[1],
but terrible is his left hand.

热词天地

1.gentle ['dʒentl] *adj.* 温和的；文雅的

神的右手是慈爱的，
左手却很可怕。

10

The world loved man when he smiled.
The world became afraid of him when he laughed.

人们微笑时，世界热爱他。
人们大笑时，世界惧怕他。

11

My heart, with its lapping[1] waves of song,
longs to caress this green world of the sunny day.

热词天地

lap [læp] *vt.* 折叠；包裹

我的心，在层叠的歌声中，
渴望着爱抚这个阳光下的绿色世界。

12

God waits for man to regain[1] his childhood in wisdom.

热词天地

1. regain [rɪ'geɪn] *vt.* 复得；重回

神等待着人在智慧中重拾童年。

13

Let me feel this world as thy love taking form,
then my love will help it.

热词天地

take form 成形

让我感觉这世界是来自您爱的创造吧，
那么，我的爱也将有助于它。

14

God kisses the finite[1] in his love and man the infinite.

热词天地

1. finite ['faɪnaɪt] *adj.* 有限的

神在他的爱里吻着"有涯",而人却吻着"无涯"。

15

Let this be my last word, that I trust thy love.

这是我的最后一句话:"我相信你的爱。"

流萤集

1

Love remains a secret even when spoken,
for only a lover truly knows that he is loved.

即使说出口来,爱情仍然是个秘密,
因为只有爱人才真正明白他是被爱着的。

2

History slowly smothers its truth,
but hastily struggles to revive it
in the terrible penance of pain.

历史慢慢扼杀了自身的真相,
然后在极度痛苦的救赎中
忙不迭地想去复活它。

3

My mind has its true union with thee, O Sky
at the window which is mine own,
and not in the open
where thou hast thy sole kingdom.

天空啊,我的心真正与你交融的地点,
是我自己的那扇窗户,
不是开阔的太空,
那是你独占的王国。

4

God loves to see in me, not his servant,
but himself who serves all.

上帝不愿我做他的仆人，
而是为众人服务的他自己。

5

The darkness of night is in harmony with day,
the morning of mist is discordant.

夜的黑暗与白昼是和谐的，
而雾气迷漾的早晨却与它不谐调。

6

The shade of my tree is for passers-by,
its fruit for the one for whom I wait.

我的树为过客留下荫凉,
它的果实要留给我等待的那个人。

7

Flushed with the glow of sunset
earth seems like a ripe fruit
ready to be harvested by night.

在落日余晖的映照下,
晕生双颊的大地,
就像一枚成熟的果实,
等待夜晚的采撷。

8

Beauty smiles in the confinement of the bud,
in the heart of a sweet incompleteness.

在花苞的囚牢里，在甜蜜的不完美里，
美莞尔而笑。

9

Your flitting love lightly brushed with its wings my sun-flower
and never asked flit was ready to surrender its honey.

你倏忽来去的爱意用翅膀轻轻拂拭
我的向日葵,
从来不曾问起,它是否愿意献出自己的花蜜。

10

Between the shores of Me and Thee
there is the loud ocean, my own
surging self,
which I long to cross.

我渴望渡过
将你我分隔两岸的
那片沸腾的海洋,那个汹涌澎湃的自我。

11

True end is not in the reaching of the
limit,
but in a completion which is limitless.

真正的完满不在于到达极限,
而在于成就无限。

12

As the tree its leaves, I shed my words on the earth.
Let my thoughts unuttered flower in thy silence.

如同树木会落叶，我将我的话语留给了大地，
让我的思绪在你的沉默中讲不出花语。

13

My faith in truth, my vision of the perfect
help thee. Master, in thy creation.

主啊，但愿我对真理的信念，对完美的领悟，
帮助你创造万物。

园丁集 （冰心 译）

1

Infinite wealth is not yours, my patient and dusky[1] mother dust!

You toil to fill the mouths of your children, but food is scarce.

The gift of gladness that you have for us is never perfect.

The toys that you make for your children are fragile.

You cannot satisfy all our hungry hopes, but should I desert[2] you for that?

Your smile which is shadowed with pain is sweet to my eyes.

Your love which knows not fulfilment is dear to my heart.

From your breast you have fed us with life but not immortality, that is why your eyes are ever wakeful³.

For ages you are working with colour and song, yet your heaven is not built, but only its sad suggestion.

Over your creations of beauty there is the mist of tears.

I will pour my songs into your mute⁴ heart, and my love into your love.

I will worship you with labour.

I have seen your tender face and I love your mournful dust, Mother Earth.

热词天地

1. dusky ['dʌskɪ] *adj.* 昏暗的，黑暗的
2. desert ['dezət] *v.* 丢开，抛弃
3. wakeful ['weɪkfl] *adj.* 失眠的；不能入睡的
4. mute [mju:t] *vt.* 减轻（声音）；使……柔和
   feed with 喂养

无量的财富不是你的,我的耐心的微黑的尘土母亲。

你操劳着来填满你孩子的嘴,但是粮食是很少的。

你给我们的欢乐礼物,永远不是完全的。

你给孩子们做的玩具,是不牢的。

你不能满足我们的一切渴望,但是我能为此就背弃你吗?

你的含着痛苦阴影的微笑,对我的眼睛是甜柔的。

你的永不满足的爱,对我的心是亲切的。

从你的胸乳里,你是以生命而不是以不朽来哺育我们,因此你的眼睛永远是警醒的。

累年积代地你用颜色和诗歌来工作,但是你的天堂还没有盖起,仅有天堂的愁苦的意味。

你的美的创造上蒙着泪雾。

我将把我的诗歌倾注入你无言的心里,把我的爱倾注入你的爱中。

我将用劳动来礼拜你。

我看见过你的温慈的面庞,我爱你的悲哀的尘土,大地母亲。

2

My heart, the bird of the wilderness, has found its sky in your eyes.

They are the cradle[1] of the morning, they are the kingdom of the stars.

My songs are lost in their depths.

Let me but soar[2] in that sky, in its lonely immensity[3].

Let me but cleave[4] its clouds and spread wings in its sunshine.

热词天地

1.cradle ['kreɪdl] *n.* 摇篮；发源地
2.soar [sɔ:(r)] *vi.* 高飞；飞腾；猛增 *vt.* 高飞越过
3.immensity [ɪ'mensətɪ] *n.* 无限，广大，巨大
4.cleave [kli:v] *n.* 劈开；紧贴；迅速穿过

我的心,这只荒野之鸟,在你的眼睛中发现了天空。
它们是早上的摇篮,它们是群星的王国。
我的歌都迷失在它们的深渊里。
就让我在那片天空中飞翔,在它孤寂的浩瀚中。
就让我穿越它的云层,在它的阳光中展开双翼。

吉檀迦利 （冰心 译）

O Fool

O Fool, try to carry thyself upon thy own shoulders! O beggar, to come beg at thy own door!

Leave all thy burdens[1] on his hands who can bear all, and never look behind in regret[2].

Thy desire at once puts out the light from the lamp it touches with its breath. It is unholy—take not thy gifts through its unclean hands. Accept only what is offered by sacred[3] love.

热词天地

1. burden ['bɜːdn] vt. 使烦恼，劳累；向（车，船等）上装货
2. regret [rɪ'gret] vt. 后悔；遗憾，抱歉；哀悼
3. sacred ['seɪkrɪd] adj. 神圣的；宗教的；受崇敬的，值得崇敬的

呵，傻子

呵，傻子，试图把自己背在肩上！呵，乞丐，来到你自己门口乞讨吧！把你的负担卸在那双能担当一切的手中，永远不要后悔地回头。

你欲望的气息会很快把它接触到的灯火吹灭。它是不圣洁的——不要从它不干净的手里接受礼物。只接受神圣的爱所付予的东西吧。

Give Me Strength

This is my prayer to thee, my lord—strike, strike at the root of penury[1] in my heart.

Give me the strength lightly to bear my joys and sorrows.

Give me the strength to make my love fruitful in service.

Give me the strength never to disown[2] the poor or bend my knees before insolent[3] might.

Give me the strength to raise my mind high above daily trifles.

And give me the strength to surrender my strength to thy will with love.

热词天地

1. penury ['penjərɪ] n. 赤贫，缺乏
2. disown [dɪs'əʊn] vt. 否认
3. insolent ['ɪnsələnt] adj. 傲慢的，无礼的

赐予我力量

这是我对你的祈求，我的主——请你铲除，铲除我心里贫乏的根源。
赐给我力量使我能轻闲地承受欢乐与忧伤。
赐给我力量使我的爱在服务中得到果实。
赐给我力量使我永不抛弃穷人也永不向淫威屈膝。
赐给我力量使我的心灵超越于日常琐事之上。
再赐给我力量使我满怀爱意地把我的力量服从你意志的指挥。

Face to Face

Day after day, O lord of my life, shall I stand before thee face to face. With folded hands, O lord of all worlds, shall I stand before thee face to face.

Under thy great sky in solitude[1] and silence, with humble heart shall I stand before thee face to face.

In this laborious world of thine, tumultuous[2] with toil and with struggle, among hurrying crowds shall I stand before thee face to face.

And when my work shall be done in this world, O, King of kings, alone and speechless shall I stand before thee face to face.

热词天地

1. solitude ['sɒlɪtjuːd] *n.* 单独，孤独；偏僻处，隐居处
2. tumultuous [tjuːˈmʌltʃuəs] *adj.* 骚乱的；吵闹的；狂暴的；激烈的

面对面

过了一天又是一天,呵,我生命的主,我能够和你面对面站立吗?呵,全世界的主,我能合掌和你面对面站立吗?

在广阔的天空下,严静之中,我能够带着虔恭的心,和你面对面站立吗?

在你的劳碌的世界里,喧腾着劳作和奋斗,在营营扰扰的人群中,我能和你面对面站立吗?

当我已做完了今生的工作,呵,万王之王,我能够独自悄立在你的面前吗?

Beggarly Heart

When the heart is hard and parched[1] up, come upon me with a shower of mercy.

When grace is lost from life, come with a burst[2] of song.

When tumultuous work raises its din on all sides shutting me out from beyond, come to me, my lord of silence, with thy peace and rest.

When my beggarly heart sits crouched[3], shut up in a corner, break open the door, my king, and come with the ceremony[4] of a king.

When desire blinds the mind with delusion and dust, O thou holy one, thou wakeful, come with thy light and thy thunder.

热词天地

1. parch [pɑːtʃ] vt. & vi. （使）焦干，（使）干透
2. burst [bɜːst] n. 爆炸；爆裂；爆发
3. crouch [kraʊtʃ] vt. 低头，屈膝
4. ceremony ['serəmənɪ] n. 典礼，仪式；礼仪，礼节

    shut out 排除，把……关在外边

赤贫之心

在我的心坚硬焦躁的时候,请洒我慈霖。

当生命失去恩宠的时候,请赐我以欢歌。

当烦躁的工作在四围喧闹,使我和外界隔绝的时候,我的宁静的主,请带着你的和平与安息来临。

当我乞丐似的心,蹲闭在屋角的时候,我的国王,请你以王者的威仪破户而入。

当欲念以诱惑与尘埃来迷蒙我的心眼的时候,呵,圣者,你是清醒的,请你和你的雷电一同降临。

Pluck This Little Flower

Pluck[1] this little flower and take it, delay not! I fear lest it droop and drop into the dust.

I may not find a place in thy garland[2], but honour it with a touch of pain from thy hand and pluck it. I fear lest the day end before I am aware, and the time of offering go by.

Though its colour be not deep and its smell be faint, use this flower in thy service and pluck it while there is time.

热词天地
1. pluck [plʌk] *n.* 勇气，精神 *vt.* 采，摘；拔掉
2. garland ['gɑ:lənd] *n.* 花环，花冠，花圈

采下这朵小花

采下这朵小花,把它拿走吧,不要迟疑!我怕它会枯萎,掉在尘土里。

它也许配不上你的花冠,但请你采摘它,以你手采摘的痛苦来给它殊荣。我怕我在察觉之前,日光流逝之时,贡献的时间也过了。

虽然它的颜色不深,香气很淡,用这朵花来礼拜吧,趁着还有时间,来采摘吧。

I Am Only Waiting for Love

I am only waiting for love to give myself up at last into his hands. That is why it is so late and why I have been guilty of such omissions.

They come with their laws and their codes to bind me fast; but I evade them ever, for I am only waiting for love to give myself up at last into his hands.

People blame me and call me heedless; I doubt not they are right in their blame.

The market day is over and work is all done for the busy. Those who came to call me in vain have gone back in anger. I am only waiting for love to give myself up at last into his hands.

我只等候着爱

我只在等候着爱,要最终把我交在他手里。这是我迟误的原因,我对这延误负咎。

他们要用法律和规章,来紧紧地约束我;但是我总是躲着他们,因为我只等候着爱,要最终把我交在他手里。

人们责备我,说我不理会人;我也知道他们的责备是有道理的。

市集已过,忙人的工作都已完毕。叫我不应的人都已含怒回去。我只等候着爱,要最终把我交在他手里。

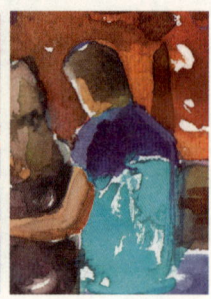

Freedom Is All I Want

Obstinate are the trammels, but my heart aches when I try to break them.
Freedom is all I want, but to hope for it I feel ashamed.

I am certain that priceless wealth is in thee, and that thou art my best friend, but I have not the heart to sweep away the tinsel that fills my room.

The shroud that covers me is a shroud of dust and death; I hate it, yet hug it in love.

My debts are large, my failures great, my shame secret and heavy; yet when I come to ask for my good, I quake in fear lest my prayer be granted.

我只要自由

罗网是坚韧的,但是要撕破它的时候我又心痛。
我只要自由,为希望自由我却觉得羞愧。

我确知那无价之宝是在你那里,而且你是我最好的朋友,但我却舍不得清除我满屋的俗物。

我身上披的是尘灰与死亡之衣;我恨它,却又热爱地把它抱紧。

我的债负很多,我的失败很大,我的耻辱秘密而又深重;但当我来求福的时候,我又战栗,唯恐我的祈求得了允诺。

Prisoner, Tell Me

"Prisoner, tell me, who was it that bound you?"

"It was my master," said the prisoner. "I thought I could outdo everybody in the world in wealth and power, and I amassed in my own treasure-house the money due to my king. When sleep overcame me I lay upon the bad that was for my lord, and on waking up I found I was a prisoner in my own treasure-house."

"Prisoner, tell me, who was it that wrought this unbreakable chain?"

"It was I," said the prisoner, "who forged this chain very carefully. I thought my invincible power would hold the world captive leaving me in a freedom undisturbed. Thus night and day I worked at the chain with huge fires and cruel hard strokes. When at last the work was done and the links were complete and unbreakable, I found that it held me in its grip."

囚人，告诉我

"囚人，告诉我，谁把你捆起来的？"

"是我的主人，"囚人说。"我以为我的财富与权力胜过世界上一切的人，我把我的国王的钱财聚敛在自己的宝库里。我昏困不过，睡在我主的床上，一觉醒来，我发现我在自己的宝库里做了囚人。"

"囚人，告诉我，是谁铸的这条坚牢的锁链？"

"是我，"囚人说，"是我自己用心铸造的。我以为我的无敌的权力会征服世界，使我有无碍的自由。我日夜用烈火重锤打造了这条铁链。等到工作完成，铁链坚牢完善，我发现这铁链把我捆住了。"

Let My Country Awake

Where the mind is without fear and the head is held high;
Where knowledge is free;

Where the world has not been broken up into fragments by narrow domestic walls;
Where words come out from the depth of truth;

Where tireless striving stretches its arms towards perfection;
Where the clear stream of reason has not lost its way into the dreary desert sand of dead habit;

Where the mind is led forward by thee into ever-widening thought and action—
Into that heaven of freedom, my Father, let my country awake.

让我的国家觉醒吧

在那里,心是无畏的,头也抬得高昂;
在那里,知识是自由的;

在那里,世界还没有被狭小的家国的墙隔成片段;
在那里,话是从真理的深处说出;

在那里,不懈的努力向着"完美"伸臂;
在那里,理智的清泉没有沉没在积习的荒漠之中;

在那里,心灵是受你的指引,走向那不断放宽的思想与行为——
进入那自由的天国,我的父呵,让我的国家觉醒起来罢。

That I Want Thee, Only Thee

That I want thee, only thee—let my heart repeat without end. All desires that distract me, day and night, are false and empty to the core.

As the night keeps hidden in its gloom the petition for light, even thus in the depth of my unconsciousness rings the cry—"I want thee, only thee".

As the storm still seeks its end in peace when it strikes against peace with all its might, even thus my rebellion strikes against thy love and still its cry is—"I want thee, only thee".

我需要你，只需要你

我需要你，只需要你——让我的心不停地重述这句话。日夜引诱我的种种欲念，都是透顶的诈伪与空虚。

就像黑夜隐藏在祈求光明的朦胧里，在我潜意识的深处也响出呼声——我需要你，只需要你。

正如风暴用全力来冲击平静，却寻求终止于平静，我的反抗冲击着你的爱，而它的呼声也还是——我需要你，只需要你。

面对面

Call Back, My Lord

The rain has held back for days and days, my God, in my arid heart.

The horizon is fiercely naked—not the thinnest cover of a soft cloud, not the vaguest hint of a distant cool shower.

Send thy angry storm, dark with death, if it is thy wish, and with lashes of lightning startle the sky from end to end.

But call back, my lord, call back this pervading silent heat, still and keen and cruel, burning the heart with dire despair.

Let the cloud of grace bend low from above like the tearful look of the mother on the day of the father's wrath.

请你召回,我的主

在我干枯的心上,好多天没有受到雨水的滋润了,我的上帝。
天边是可怕的赤裸——没有一片轻云的遮盖,没有一丝远雨的凉意。

如果你愿意,请降下你的死黑的盛怒的风雨,以闪电震慑诸天罢。

但是请你召回,我的主,召回这弥漫沉默的炎热罢,它是沉重尖锐而又残忍的,用可怕的绝望焚灼人心。

让慈云低垂下降,像在父亲发怒的时候,母亲的含泪的眼光。

The Baby

The sleep that flits on baby's eyes—does anybody know from where it comes? Yes, there is a rumour that it has its dwelling where, in the fairy village among shadows of the forest dimly lit with glow-worms, there hang two timid buds of enchantment. From there it comes to kiss baby's eyes.

The smile that flickers on baby's lips when he sleeps—does anybody know where it was born? Yes, there is a rumour that a young pale beam of a crescent moon touched the edge of a vanishing autumn cloud, and there the smile was first born in the dream of a dew-washed morning—the smile that flickers on baby's lips when he sleeps.

The sweet, soft freshness that blooms on baby's limbs—does anybody know where it was hidden so long? Yes, when the mother was a young girl it lay pervading her heart in tender and silent mystery of love—the sweet, soft freshness that has bloomed on baby's limbs.

婴儿

这掠过婴儿眼上的睡眠——有谁知道它是从哪里来的吗?是的,有谣传说它住在林荫中,萤火朦胧照着的仙村里,那里挂着两颗甜柔迷人的花蕾。它从那里来吻着婴儿的眼睛。

在婴儿睡梦中唇上闪现的微笑——有谁知道它是从哪里生出来的吗?是的,有谣传说一线新月的微笑,触到了消散的秋云的边缘,微笑就在被朝雾洗净的晨梦中,第一次生出来了——这就是那婴儿睡梦中唇上闪现的微笑。

在婴儿的四肢上,花朵般地喷发的甜柔清新的生气,有谁知道它是在哪里藏了这么许久吗?是的,当母亲还是一个少女,它就在温柔安静的爱的神秘中,充塞在她的心里了——这就是那婴儿四肢上喷发的甜柔新鲜的生气。

I Do Not Know Thee As My Own

I know thee as my God and stand apart—I do not know thee as my own and come closer. I know thee as my father and bow before thy feet—I do not grasp thy hand as my friend's.

I stand not where thou comest down and ownest thyself as mine, there to clasp thee to my heart and take thee as my comrade.

Thou art the Brother amongst my brothers, but I heed them not, I divide not my earnings with them, thus sharing my all with thee.

In pleasure and in pain I stand not by the side of men, and thus stand by thee. I shrink to give up my life, and thus do not plunge into the great waters of life.

我不知道你是属于我的

我知道你是我的上帝,却远立在一边——我不知道你是属于我的,就走近你。我知道你是我的父亲,就在你脚前俯伏——我没有像和朋友握手那样地紧握你的手。

我没有在你降临的地方,站立等候,把你抱在胸前,当你做同志,把你占有。

你是我弟兄的弟兄,但是我不理他们,不把我赚得的和他们平分,我以为这样做,才能和你分享我的一切。

在快乐和苦痛里,我都没有站在人类的一边,我以为这样做,才能和你站在一起。我畏缩着不肯舍生,因此我没有跳入生命的伟大的海洋里。

Where Had They Hid Their Power?

When the warriors came out first from their master's hall, where had they hid their power? Where were their armour and their arms?

They looked poor and helpless, and the arrows were showered upon them on the day they came out from their master's hall.

When the warriors marched back again to their master's hall where did they hide their power?

They had dropped the sword and dropped the bow and the arrow; peace was on their foreheads, and they had left the fruits of their life behind them on the day they marched back again to their master's hall.

他们的武力藏在哪里呢?

当战士们从他们主公的明堂里刚走出来,他们的武力藏在哪里呢?他们的甲胄和干戈藏在哪里呢?

他们显得无助、可怜,当他们从他们主公的明堂走出的那一天,如雨的箭矢向着他飞射。

当战士们整队走回他们主公的明堂里的时候,他们的武力藏在哪里呢?

他们放下了刀剑和弓矢;和平在他们的额上放光,当他们整队走回他们主公的明堂的那一天,他们把他们生命的果实留在后面了。

Death

Death, thy servant, is at my door. He has crossed the unknown sea and brought thy call to my home.

The night is dark and my heart is fearful—yet I will take up the lamp, open my gates and bow to him my welcome. It is thy messenger who stands at my door.

I will worship him placing at his feet the treasure of my heart.

He will go back with his errand done, leaving a dark shadow on my morning; and in my desolate home only my forlorn self will remain as my last offering to thee.

死亡

　　死亡，你的仆人，来到我的门前。他渡过不可知的海洋临到我家，来传达你的召令。

　　夜色沉黑，我心中畏惧——但是我要端起灯来，开起门来，鞠躬欢迎他。因为站在我门前的是你的使者。

　　我要把我心中的财产，放在他脚前，来礼拜他。

　　他的使命完成了就要回去，在我的晨光中留下了阴影；在我萧条的家里，只剩下孤独的我，作为最后献你的祭品。

面对面

I Will Never Shut the Doors of My Senses

Deliverance is not for me in renunciation. I feel the embrace of freedom in a thousand bonds of delight.

Thou ever pourest for me the fresh draught of thy wine of various colours and fragrance, filling this earthen vessel to the brim.

My world will light its hundred different lamps with thy flame and place them before the altar of thy temple.

No, I will never shut the doors of my senses. The delights of sight and hearing and touch will bear thy delight.

Yes, all my illusions will burn into illumination of joy, and all my desires ripen into fruits of love.

我永不会关上我感觉的门户

在断念屏欲之中,我不需要拯救。在万千欢愉的约束里我感到了自由的拥抱。

你不断地向我的瓦罐里满满地斟上不同颜色不同芬芳的新酒。
我的世界,将以你的火焰点上他的万盏不同的明灯,安放在你庙宇的坛前。

不,我永不会关上我感觉的门户。视、听、触的快乐会含带着你的快乐。

是的,我的一切幻想会燃烧成快乐的光明,我的一切愿望将结成爱的果实。

第五卷
最后的帷幕

飞鸟集

1

While the glass lamp rebukes[1] the earthen for calling it cousin the moon rises,
and the glass lamp, with a bland[2] smile, calls her,
—My dear, dear sister.

热词天地

1.rebuke [rɪ'bjuːk] *vt.* 非难，指责；制止，阻止
2.bland [blænd] *adj.* 温和的，和蔼的；平和的

玻璃灯因为瓦灯称其表兄而责备它，
当明月出来时，玻璃灯却莞尔一笑，
叫明月为——我亲爱的，亲爱的姐姐。

2

We come nearest to the great when we are great in humility[1].

热词天地

1.humility [hjuːˈmɪlətɪ] *n.* 谦逊；谦恭

我们最为谦卑的时候，也是最接近伟大的时候。

3

Wrong cannot afford defeat[1] but Right can.

热词天地

1.defeat [dɪˈfiːt] *n.* 战胜；失败

错误经不起失败，但是真理却可以。

4

We read the world wrong and say that it deceives[1] us.

热词天地

1.deceive [dɪ'siːv] *v.* 欺诈;误导

我们看错了世界,却说它欺骗了我们。

5

The echo mocks[1] her origin to prove she is the original.

热词天地

1.mock [mɒk] *vt.* & *vi.* 愚弄,嘲弄

回音嘲笑她的原声,以证明她是最初的声音。

6

The power that boasts of its mischiefs is laughed at by the yellow leaves that fall, and clouds that pass by.

热词天地

boast of 夸耀，吹嘘

权势吹嘘着它的淫威，金黄的落叶和漂浮的流云却在笑它。

7

The water in a vessel[1] is sparkling;
the water in the sea is dark.
The small truth has words that are clear;
the great truth has great silence.

热词天地

1.vessel ['vesl] *n.* 容器；船，飞船

杯中之水闪耀光辉；
海中之水却一片漆黑。
小道理可以用文字言明；
大道理却只有沉默。

8

If you shut your door to all errors truth will be shut out.

当你把所有的错误都关在门外时,
真理也被挡在外面了。

9

By plucking[1] her petals[2] you do not gather the beauty of the flower.

热词天地
1.pluck [plʌk] *vt.* 采,摘
2.petal ['petl] *n.* 花瓣

采摘花瓣时,得不到花儿的美丽。

10

He who is too busy doing good finds no time to be good.

太急于做好事的人,反而无暇做好人。

11

Kicks only raise dust and not crops[1] from the earth.

热词天地

1.crop [krɒp] *vt.* 种植;收割

踢足不能从地上获得收获,惟有扬起尘土。

12

The stream of truth flows through its channels[1] of mistakes.

热词天地
1.channel ['tʃænl] *n.* 渠道

真理之川从错误之渠中流淌。

13

Let him only see the thorns who has eyes to see the rose.

让那些看到玫瑰花的人也只看它的刺吧。

14

We live in this world when we love it.

我们热爱这个世界,便生活在这里。

15

The false can never grow into truth by growing in power.

热词天地

grow into 成长为……

成长于权力之中的虚伪,永远不能变成真实。

最后的帷幕

流萤集

1

My fancies are fireflies,—
Specks of living light
twinkling in the dark.

我的幻想是一群萤火虫，——
是星星点点的流光
在黑暗中闪现。

2

The voice of wayside pansies,
 that do not attract the careless glance,
murmurs in these desultory lines.

路边的紫罗兰,
吸引不了这无心的目光,
它的声音却在这些散乱的诗间呢喃。

3

In the drowsy dark caves of the mind
 dreams build their nest with fragments
dropped from day's caravan.

在沉寂慵倦的心的洞穴里,
梦用白天在旅行中遗落的花瓣
筑起自己的巢窠。

4

Spring scatters the petals of flowers,
that are not for the fruits of the future
but for the moment's whim.

春天散播这些花瓣，
不是为了将来结成果实，
只是为了一时的妄想。

5

Joy freed from the bond of earth's slumber
rushes into numbefless leaves,
and dances in the air for a day.

喜悦从大地的梦寐中解放出来，
涌入这无尽的繁枝密叶中，
终日在空中欢快起舞。

6

My words that are slight
may lightly dance upon time's waves
when my works heavy with import have
gone down.

当我的那些载满沉重意义的鸿篇已然消逝时，
我那些轻灵琐碎的文字
或许依然在时光的波涛上翩跹。

7

From the solemn gloom of the temple
children run out to sit in the dust,
God watches them play
and forgets the priest.

孩子们跑出庄严肃穆的神庙，
在尘灰中坐下，
上帝看着他们嬉戏玩耍，
却忘记了那个祭司。

8

My mind starts up at some flash
on the flow of its thoughts,
like a brook at a sudden liquid note of its own
that is never repeated.

如思绪流动中一闪的光亮,
我的心遽然惊动,
宛如潺潺溪流惊讶于水声里
那一个永不再现的音符。

9

Maiden, thy beauty is like a fruit
which is yet to mature,
tense with an unyielding secret.

少女啊,你的美丽就像
一枚尚未成熟的果实,
带着倔强的秘密而紧张。

10

Sorrow that has lost its memory
is like the dumb dark hours
that have no bird songs
but only the cricket's chirp.

失去记忆的哀伤
如同暗哑的黑暗时光,
没有鸟儿的欢唱,
只剩下蟋蟀的低鸣。

园丁集 （冰心 译）

1

I run as a musk-deer[1] runs in the shadow of the forest mad with his own perfume[2].

The night is the night of mid-May, the breeze is the breeze of the south.

I lose my way and I wander, I seek what I cannot get, I get what I do not seek.

From my heart comes out and dances the image of my own desire.
The gleaming vision flits on.
I try to clasp it firmly, it eludes[3] me and leads me astray[4].
I seek what I cannot get, I get what I do not seek.

热词天地

1.musk-deer [ˈmʌskdˈɪər] *n.* [医] 麝
2.perfume [ˈpɜːfjuːm] *n.* 香水；香料
3.elude [ɪˈluːd] *vt.* 逃避；使……迷惑
4.astray [əˈstreɪ] *adv.* 迷路地；堕落，误入歧途地

我像麝鹿一样在林荫中奔走,为着自己的香气而发狂。

夜晚是五月正中的夜晚,清风是南国的清风。

我迷了路,我游荡着,我寻求那得不到的东西,我得到我所没有寻求的东西。

我自己的愿望的形象从我心中走出,跳起舞来。

我闪光的形象飞掠过去。

我想把它紧紧捉住,它躲开了又引着我飞走下去。

我寻求那得不到的东西,我得到我所没有寻求的东西。

2

The tame[1] bird was in a cage, the free bird was in the forest.
They met when the time came, it was a decree[2] of fate.

The free bird cries, "O my love, let us fly to wood."
The cage bird whispers, "Come hither[3], let us both live in the cage."

Says the free bird, "Among bars, where is there room to spread one's wings?"
"Alas," cries the cage bird, "I should not know where to sit perched[4] in the sky."

The free bird cries, "My darling, sing the songs of the woodlands."
The cage bird says, "Sit by my side, I'll teach you the speech of the learned."

The forest bird cries, "No, ah no! Songs can never be taught."

The cage bird says, "Alas for me, I know not the songs of the woodlands."

Their love is intense[5] with longing, but they never can fly wing to wing.

Through the bars of the cage they look, and vain is their wish to know each other.

They flutter their wings in yearning, and sing, "Come closer, my love!"

The free bird cries, "It cannot be, I fear the closed doors of the cage."

The cage bird whispers, "Alas, my wings are powerless and dead."

热词天地

1. tame [teɪm] *adj.* 驯服的；平淡的
2. decree [dɪˈkriː] *n.* 法令，命令
3. hither [ˈhɪðə(r)] *adv.* <古> 到此处，向此处
4. perch [pɜːtʃ] *vt.* & *vi.* 栖息；停留
5. intense [ɪnˈtens] *adj.* 热情的；强烈的

驯养的鸟在笼里,自由的鸟在林中。
时间到了,他们相会,这是命中注定的。

自由的鸟说:"呵,我的爱,让我们飞到林中去吧。"
笼中的鸟低声说:"到这里来吧,让我俩都住在笼里。"

自由的鸟说:"在栅栏中间,哪有展翅的余地呢?"
"可怜呵,"笼中的鸟说,"在天空中我不晓得到哪里去栖息。"

自由的鸟叫唤说:"我的宝贝,唱起林野之歌吧。"
笼中的鸟说:"坐在我旁边吧,我要教你说学者的语言。"

自由的鸟叫唤说:"不,不!歌曲是不能传授的。"
笼中的鸟说:"可怜的我呵,我不会唱林野之歌。"

他们的爱情因渴望而更加热烈,但是他们永不能比翼双飞。
他们隔栏相望,而他们相知的愿望是虚空的。
他们在依恋中振翼,唱说:"靠近些吧,我的爱!"

自由的鸟叫唤说:"这是做不到的,我怕这笼子的紧闭的门。"
笼里的鸟低声说:"我的翅翼是无力的,而且已经死去了。"

3

A wandering madman was seeking the touchstone[1], with matted locks tawny[2] and dust-laden, and body worn to a shadow, his lips tight-pressed, like the shut-up doors of his heart, his burning eyes like the lamp of a glow-worm seeking its mate.

Before him the endless ocean roared.

The garrulous waves ceaselessly talked of hidden treasures, mocking the ignorance that knew not their meaning.

Maybe he now had no hope remaining, yet he would not rest, for the search had become his life—

Just as the ocean for ever lifts its arms to the sky for the unattainable—

Just as the stars go in circles, yet seeking a goal that can never be reached—

Even so on the lonely shore the madman with dusty tawny locks still roamed in search of the touchstone.

One day a village boy came up and asked, "Tell me, where did you come at this golden chain about your waist?"

The madman started—the chain that once was iron was verily[3] gold; it was not a dream, but he did not know when it had changed.

He struck his forehead wildly—where, O where had he without knowing it achieved success?

It had grown into a habit, to pick up pebbles and touch the chain, and to throw them away without looking to see if a change had come; thus the madman found and lost the touchstone.

The sun was sinking low in the west, the sky was of gold.

The madman returned on his footsteps to seek anew the lost treasure, with his strength gone, his body bent, and his heart in the dust, like a tree uprooted.

热词天地

1. touchstone ['tʌtʃstəʊn] *n.* 试金石；（检验）标准
2. tawny ['tɔ:nɪ] *adj.* 黄褐色的
3. verily ['verɪlɪ] *adv.* 真实地，真正地

for ever 永远，总是
in search of 寻找
grow into 成长为……

一个流浪的疯子在寻找点金石。他褐黄的头发乱蓬蓬地蒙着尘土，身体瘦得像个影子。他双唇紧闭，就像他的紧闭的心门。他的烧红的眼睛就像萤火虫的灯亮在寻找它的爱侣。

无边的海在他面前怒吼。

喧哗的波浪，在不停地谈论那隐藏的珠宝，嘲笑那不懂得它们的意思的愚人。

也许现在他不再有希望了，但是他不肯休息，因为寻求变成他的生命——

就像海洋永远向天伸臂要求不可得到的东西——

就像星辰绕着圈走，却要寻找一个永不能到达的目标——

在那寂寞的海边，那头发垢乱的疯子，也仍旧徘徊着寻找点金石。

有一天，一个村童走上来问："告诉我，你腰上的那条金链是从哪里来的呢？"

疯子吓了一跳——那条本来是铁的链子真的变成金的了；这不是一场梦，但是他不知道是什么时候变成的。

他狂乱地敲着自己的前额——什么时候，呵，什么时候在他的不知不觉之中得到成功了呢？

拾起小石去碰碰那条链子，然后不看看变化与否，又把它扔掉，这已成了习惯；就是这样，这疯子找到了又失掉了那块点金石。

太阳西沉，天空灿金。

疯子沿着自己的脚印走回，去寻找他失去的珍宝。他力气尽消，身体弯曲，他的心像连根拔起的树一样，萎垂在尘土里了。

吉檀迦利 （冰心 译）

Purity

Life of my life, I shall ever try to keep my body pure, knowing that thy living touch is upon all my limbs.

I shall ever try to keep all untruths out from my thoughts, knowing that thou art that truth which has kindled the light of reason in my mind.

I shall ever try to drive all evils away from my heart and keep my love in flower, knowing that thou hast thy seat in the inmost shrine of my heart.

And it shall be my endeavour[1] to reveal thee in my actions, knowing it is thy power gives me strength to act.

热词天地

1.endeavour [ɪnˈdevə(r)] n. 尽力，竭力
　drive away 驱车离开；把……驱开，赶走

纯洁

我生命的生命,我要保持我的躯体永远纯洁,因为我知道你的生命摩抚,接触着我的四肢。

我要永远从我的思想中屏除虚伪,因为我知道你就是那在我心中燃起理智之火的真理。

我要从我心中驱走一切的丑恶,使我的爱开花,因为我知道你在我的心宫深处安设了座位。

我要努力在我的行为上表现你,因为我知道是你的威力,给我力量来行动。

The Last Curtain

I know that the day will come when my sight of this earth shall be lost, and life will take its leave in silence, drawing the last curtain over my eyes.

Yet stars will watch at night, and morning rise as before, and hours heave[1] like sea waves casting up pleasures and pains.

When I think of this end of my moments, the barrier of the moments breaks and I see by the light of death thy world with its careless treasures. Rare is its lowliest seat, rare[2] is its meanest of lives.

Things that I longed for in vain and things that I got—let them pass. Let me but truly possess the things that I ever spurned[3] and overlooked.

热词天地

1.heave [hi:v] *vt.* 举起；投掷
2.rare [reə(r)] *adj.* 罕见的；特殊的
3.spurn [spɜ:n] *vt.* 蔑视；唾弃；轻视地踏或踢
　cast up 计算，把……加起来；冲击
　long for 渴望；羡慕；憧憬

最后的帷幕

我知道这日子将要来到,当我眼中的人世渐渐消失,生命默默地向我道别,把最后的帘幕拉过我的眼前。

但是星辰将在夜中守望,晨曦仍旧升起,时间像海波的汹涌,激荡着欢乐与哀伤。

当我想到我的时间的终点,时间的隔栏便破裂了,在死的光明中,我看见了你的世界和这世界里弃置的珍宝。最低的座位是极其珍奇的,最小的生物也是世间少有的。

我追求而未得到和我已经得到的东西——让它们过去罢。只让我真正地据有那些我曾经轻视和忽略的东西。

Thy Gifts to Us Mortals

Thy gifts to us mortals fulfil all our needs and yet run back to thee undiminished.

The river has its everyday work to do and hastens through fields and hamlets; yet its incessant stream winds towards the washing of thy feet.

The flower sweetens the air with its perfume; yet its last service is to offer itself to thee.

Thy worship does not impoverish the world.

From the words of the poet men take what meanings please them; yet their last meaning points to thee.

你赐给我们世人的礼物

你赐给我们世人的礼物,满足了我们一切的需要,可是它们又毫未减少地返回到你那里。

河水有它每天的工作,匆忙地穿过田野和村庄;但它的不绝的水流,又曲折地回来洗你的双脚。

花朵以芬芳熏香了空气;但它最终的任务,是把自己献上给你。

对你供献不会使世界困穷。

人们从诗人的字句里,选取自己心爱的意义;但是诗句的最终意义是指向着你。

Who Is He?

I came out alone on my way to my tryst[1]. But who is this that follows me in the silent dark?

I move aside to avoid his presence but I escape him not.

He makes the dust rise from the earth with his swagger[2]; he adds his loud voice to every word that I utter.

He is my own little self, my lord, he knows no shame; but I am ashamed to come to thy door in his company.

热词天地

1.tryst [trɪst] *n.* <古> 约会，幽会；幽会地点
2.swagger ['swægə(r)] *n.* 昂首阔步；吹嘘，自大
　add to 增加，加强
　be ashamed to 羞于……

他是谁?

我独自去赴幽会。是谁在暗寂中跟着我呢?

我走开躲他,但是我逃不掉。

他昂首阔步,使地上尘土飞扬;我说出的每一个字里,都掺杂着他的喊叫。

他就是我的小我,我的主,他恬不知耻;但和他一同到你门前,我却感到羞愧。

Stream of Life

The same stream of life that runs through my veils night and day runs through the world and dances in rhythmic[1] measures.

It is the same life that shoots in joy through the dust of the earth in numberless blades of grass and breaks into tumultuous waves of leaves and flowers.

It is the same life that is rocked in the ocean-cradle of birth and of death, in ebb[2] and in flow.

I feel my limbs are made glorious by the touch of this world of life. And my pride is from the life-throb[3] of ages dancing in my blood this moment.

热词天地
1. rhythmic ['rɪðmɪk] *adj.* 有韵律的；有节奏的
2. ebb [eb] *vi.* （指潮水）退；跌落
3. throb [θrɒb] *n.* 脉搏；跳动

生命的溪流

就是这股生命的泉水,日夜流穿我的血管,也流穿过世界,又应节地跳舞。

就是这同一的生命,从大地的尘土里快乐地伸放出无数片的芳草,迸发出繁花密叶的波纹。

就是这同一的生命,在潮汐里摇动着生和死的大海的摇篮。

我觉得我的四肢因受着生命世界的爱抚而光荣。我的骄傲,是因为时代的脉搏,此刻在我血液中跳动。

You stood at my cottage door

You came down from your throne and stood at my cottage door.

I was singing all alone in a corner, and the melody caught your ear. You came down and stood at my cottage door.

Masters are many in your hall, and songs are sung there at all hours.

But the simple carol of this novice[1] struck at your love. One plaintive[2] little strain[3] mingled with[4] the great music of the world, and with a flower for a prize you came down and stopped at my cottage door.

热词天地

1. novice ['nɒvɪs] *n.* 初学者，新手
2. plaintive ['pleɪntɪv] *adj.* 悲哀的，哀怨的；哭诉的；可怜的
3. strain [streɪn] *n.* 血统，家族；性格；一段音乐
   mingle with 混合

你站在我的草舍门前

你从宝座下来,站到了我草舍门前。

我正在屋角独唱,歌声被你聆听。

你下来站在我草舍门前。

在你大厅里的许多名家,一天到晚都在放声高歌。

但是这初学者的简单的音乐,却得到了你的赏识。一支忧郁的小调,与世界的伟大音乐融合在一起,你带来花朵作为奖赏,下了宝座驻留在我的草舍门前。

Look Forward to You

I know not from what distant time thou art ever coming nearer to meet me.

Thy sun and stars can never keep thee hidden from me for aye.

In many a morning and eve thy footsteps have been heard and thy messenger has come within my heart and called me in secret.

I know not only why today my life is all astir, and a feeling of tremulous joy is passing through my heart.

It is as if the time were come to wind up my work, and I feel in the air a faint smell of thy sweet presence.

期待你

我不知道从永远的什么时候,你就一直走近来迎接我。

你的太阳和星辰永不能把你藏起使我看不见你。

在许多清晨和傍晚,我曾听见你的足音,你的使者曾秘密地到我心里来召唤。

我不知道为什么今天我的生活完全激动了,一种狂欢的感觉穿过了我的心。

这就像结束工作的时间已到,我感觉到在空气中有你光降的微馨。

Farewell

I have got my leave. Bid me farewell[1], my brothers! I bow[2] to you all and take my departure.

Here I give back the keys of my door—and I give up all claims to my house. I only ask for last kind words from you.

We were neighbours for long, but I received more than I could give. Now the day has dawned and the lamp that lit my dark corner is out. A summons[3] has come and I am ready for my journey.

热词天地

1. farewell ['feə'wel] *n.* 告别，欢送；欢送会
2. bow [baʊ] *vi.* （向……）弯腰；鞠躬
3. summons ['sʌmənz] *n.* 召唤
    give up 放弃；投降；把……让给；戒除
    for long 长久

辞别

我已经请了假。弟兄们,祝我一路平安罢!我向你们大家鞠了躬就启程了。

我把我门上的钥匙交还——我把房子的所有权都放弃了。我只请求你们最后的几句好话。

我们做过很久的邻居,但是我接受的多,给与的少。现在天已破晓,我黑暗屋角的灯光已灭。召命已来,我就准备启行了。

Gloaming

The day is no more, the shadow is upon the earth. It is time that I go to the stream to fill my pitcher.

The evening air is eager with the sad music of the water. Ah, it calls me out into the dusk. In the lonely lane[1] there is no passer-by, the wind is up, the ripples[2] are rampant[3] in the river.

I know not if I shall come back home. I know not whom I shall chance to meet. There at the fording in the little boat the unknown man plays upon his lute[4].

热词天地

1. lane [leɪn] *n.* 小路，小巷
2. ripple ['rɪpl] *vt.* & *vi.* 使泛起涟漪
3. rampant ['ræmpənt] *adj.* 蔓延的；猖獗的
4. lute [lu:t] *n.* 鲁特琴；封泥；古琵琶

黄昏

白日散尽,影子投于大地。是我去溪边汲水的时候了。

夜空期盼河流的哀乐。啊,它呼唤我走进苍茫暮色。荒路上人迹罕至,微风初起,河面荡起层层涟漪。

我不知是否该归家,也不知会邂逅谁。渡口的小小泊船上,一个陌生人在拨弄古琵琶。

Let Only That Little Be Left of Me

Let only that little be left of me whereby I may name thee my all.

Let only that little be left of my will whereby I may feel thee on every side, and come to thee in everything, and offer to thee my love every moment.

Let only that little be left of me whereby I may never hide thee.

Let only that little of my fetters be left whereby I am bound with thy will, and thy purpose is carried out in my life—and that is the fetter of thy love.

只要我一息尚存

只要我一息尚存，我就称你为我的一切。

只要我一诚不灭，我就感觉到你在我的四围，任何事情，我都来请教你，任何时候都把我的爱献上给你。

只要我一息尚存，我就永不把你藏匿起来。

只要把我和你的旨意锁在一起的脚镣，还留着一小段，你的意旨就在我的生命中实现——这脚镣就是你的爱。

Thou Lord of All Heavens

Thus it is that thy joy in me is so full. Thus it is that thou hast come down to me. O thou lord of all heavens, where would be thy love if I were not?

Thou hast taken me as thy partner of all this wealth. In my heart is the endless play of thy delight. In my life thy will is ever taking shape.

And for this, thou who art the King of kings hast decked thyself in beauty to captivate my heart. And for this thy love loses itself in the love of thy lover, and there art thou seen in the perfect union of two.

你这万王之王

只因你的快乐是这样的充满了我的心。只因你曾这样地俯就我。呵，你这诸天之主，假如没有我，你还爱谁呢？

你使我做了你这一切财富的共享者。在我心里你的欢乐不住地遨游。在我生命中你的意志永远实现。

因此，你这万王之王曾把自己修饰了来赢取我的心。因此你的爱也消融在你情人的爱里，在那里，你又以我俩完全合一的形象显现。

When Death Will Knock at Thy Door

On the day when death will knock at thy door what wilt thou offer to him?

Oh, I will set before my guest the full vessel of my life—I will never let him go with empty hands.

All the sweet vintage of all my autumn days and summer nights, all the earnings and gleanings of my busy life will I place before him at the close of my days when death will knock at my door.

当死神来叩你门的时候

当死神来叩你门的时候,你将以什么贡献他呢?

呵,我要在我客人面前,摆上我的满斟的生命之杯——我绝不让他空手回去。

我一切的秋日和夏夜的丰美的收获,我匆促的生命中的一切获得和收藏,在我临终,死神来叩我的门的时候,我都要摆在他的面前。